Wha
Sho

Marriage, Separation and Divorce

What Every Woman Should Know About Marriage, Separation and Divorce

Lynn King

James Lorimer & Company, Publishers
Toronto 1980

ISBN 0-88862-291-0 cloth
0-88862-290-2 paper

Design: Don Fernley
Cover Photo: Peter Paterson

6 5 4 3 2 1 80 81 82 83 84 85 86

Canadian Cataloguing in Publication Data

King, Lynn, 1945–
What every woman should know about marriage, separation and divorce

ISBN 0-88862-291-0 bd. ISBN 0-88862-290-2 pa.

1. Marriage law - Canada - Popular works.
2. Separation (Law) - Canada - Popular works.
3. Divorce - Canada - Popular works. I. Title.

KE544.Z82K55 346.7101'6 C80-094090-3

James Lorimer & Company, Publishers
Egerton Ryerson Memorial Building
35 Britain Street,
Toronto M5A 1R7, Ontario

Printed and bound in Canada

CONTENTS

Acknowledgments *11*

Introduction *13*

1. Marriage *19*

Must a wife take her husband's name? *19*
Does a wife have a right to her husband's earnings and income? *19*
Is a wife responsible for her husband's debts? *20*
Is a husband responsible for his wife's debts? *20*
Does a wife become co-owner of her husband's property or business? *20*
Does a wife inherit her husband's estate? *21*
Other rights and obligations in marriage *21*
What is the difference between being married and living together? *21*
Marriage contracts: What are they? *22*
What do marriage contracts deal with? *22*
What makes a marriage contract valid? *23*
Why enter into a marriage contract? *23*
What are the problems with marriage contracts? *24*
When will courts overlook the terms of marriage contracts? *24*

2. Marriage Breakdown *26*

Seeing a lawyer *27*

Hiring a lawyer *28*

3. Divorce *30*

Why divorce? *30*
Who can apply? *31*
How do you apply for a divorce? *32*
How will your husband learn of the petition? *32*
Must your husband reply within a certain time? *33*
Once your husband is served, what can he do? *33*
What happens before the divorce hearing? *34*

GROUNDS FOR DIVORCE *37*
Matrimonial offences *37*
Adultery *37*
Cruelty *38*
    Can a husband sue for cruelty? *43*
    How do you prove cruelty? *44*
    Must you be living separate and apart to prove cruelty? *45*
    How bad does your husband's conduct have to be? *46*
    Must your husband intend to hurt you? *46*
    What corroboration is required? *46*
Homosexual acts *48*
Other matrimonial offences *48*
Marriage breakdown *48*
Three or five years' separation *48*
Gross addiction to alcohol or narcotics *50*
Non-consummation *50*
Other circumstances *51*
If grounds are shown, can a court refuse to grant a divorce? *51*
When do you get your final divorce decree? *51*
What name can a married or divorced woman use? *52*
Who pays for the divorce? *53*

4. Child Custody and Access *55*

What does custody mean? *55*
What are the age limits in custody matters? *55*
In what province should custody be sought? *56*
Who has custody of the children before the final trial? *57*
How is final custody determined? *58*

What evidence will be used at the custody trial? *58*
The child's wishes *58*
Home study reports *59*
Psychiatric and psychological reports *59*
School and pediatric reports *61*
Neighbours, friends and sundry witnesses *61*
What will the judge consider in deciding custody? *62*
Who left the family home? *62*
Past conduct of parents *63*
How much money does each parent have? *64*
Age of children *65*
Sex of children *65*
Present conduct and living arrangements of parents *65*
Types of custody orders *69*
Separation of siblings *69*
Divided custody *69*
Joint custody *69*
Unmarried parents *69*
Custody to people other than parents *70*
Kidnapping *70*
Arbitration *70*
Can a custody order be changed? *70*
Access *71*
How is access determined? *72*
What exceptional circumstances allow denial of access? *72*
What conditions are imposed on visiting rights? *74*
Can a reluctant child be forced to visit with a parent? *74*
Access and child support *74*
May the parent with custody leave the jurisdiction? *75*
Can access be changed? *75*
Conclusion *75*

5. Property *77*

What is meant by property? *77*
Does a woman have any right to her husband's property? *77*
Dower and homestead rights *78*
Married Women's Property Acts and separate property *78*

What does separate property mean? *79*
Whose name is the property in? *79*
Who owns property the husband has given to the wife and put in her name? *80*
What rights does the wife gain through financial contribution to property in the husband's name? *80*
What rights does the wife gain through non-financial contribution to the husband's property? *81*

WHY REFORM? *83*
Family assets — Ontario, Prince Edward Island and British Columbia *83*
What are family assets? *83*
When are the family assets divided? *86*
Can the husband sell a potential family asset at the time of separation? *86*
How does the wife know what assets the husband has? *87*
In what proportion are the family assets divided? *87*
How are the family assets actually shared? *88*
What happens to non-family assets? *88*
Other ways to get non-family assets *90*
Other reform provinces — Alberta, Saskatchewan and Manitoba *91*
Alberta *92*
Saskatchewan *92*
Manitoba *93*
What happens to the family or matrimonial home? *93*
Will the wife get a share of the sale proceeds? *94*
Can the wife have her husband ordered out of the matrimonial home? *94*
What are the wife's rights to possession of the home? *95*
Conclusion *96*

6. Support and Maintenance *97*

CAN A WIFE GET SUPPORT WITHOUT GETTING A DIVORCE? *97*

Matrimonial misconduct provinces — Alberta, Saskatchewan, New Brunswick, Nova Scotia, Newfoundland and the Yukon and Northwest Territories *98*
What is desertion? *98*
Can a husband apply for support in these provinces? *99*
Alimony *99*
Wife's adultery *99*
No-fault provinces — Ontario, Prince Edward Island, British Columbia and Manitoba *100*
When can the wife bring a claim for support? *100*
How much will the wife get? *100*
How much does the wife need? *103*
How is conduct a factor in these provinces? *103*
What is the position of a working wife? *103*
What kind of orders can be made? *104*

DIVORCE AND MAINTENANCE *105*
Is conduct throughout the marriage considered? *105*
Adultery *106*
Condition, means and other circumstances *106*
Additional factors *108*
When are wives ordered to pay maintenance? *110*
Is a maintenance claim affected by a delay between separation and the divorce hearing? *111*
When will a lump-sum payment be ordered? *111*
What effect do separation agreements have on maintenance orders? *113*
What arrangements can be made until the divorce is heard? *115*
When do payments begin and how long do they continue? *116*
Can the orders be changed if financial circumstances change? *116*

CHILD SUPPORT *117*
For how long must one pay child support? *118*
Who will be ordered to pay child support? *118*
How much can be ordered? *118*

7. Separation Agreements *120*
Do you need a separation agreement? *121*
What are the advantages of a separation agreement? *123*
Terms of a separation agreement *123*
Date of separation *124*
Non-molestation, non-interference *124*
Custody and access *124*
Support *124*
Variation clause *125*
Property division *125*
Medical and hospital care *125*
Insurance *125*
Other clauses *125*
How long does the agreement last? *126*
When is a separation agreement invalid? *126*

8. Strategies and Tactics *129*

Conclusion *134*

Appendix: Sample forms and agreements *137*
Marriage contract *137*
Petition for divorce *147*
Separation agreement *157*

Glossary *165*

ACKNOWLEDGMENTS

During the course of writing this book, my mind was more often on it than on the day-to-day running of my law office. I am therefore grateful to my wonderful law partners, Mary Cornish and Harriet Sachs, for putting up with me, to say nothing of their support throughout. I am also grateful to my secretary, Victoria Midgley, who tirelessly and patiently helped me from beginning to end, and who offered useful suggestions and insights all along.

I have often thought of writing a book like this but would never have actually done so without the encouragement and help of James Lorimer, whom I thank. I, of course, take full responsibility for its shortcomings.

L.K.

INTRODUCTION

Women have been shortchanged, and nowhere is this more evident than in marriage, separation and divorce. Because of their weak economic position and relative lack of experience in the business world, women are at a distinct disadvantage when it comes to operating as equal partners in marriage and equal negotiators when a marriage dissolves.

Although we now have all sorts of family legislation that makes claims to equality, women learn only too late that these are mostly just words. One Ontario statute states in its preamble:

> It is necessary to recognize the equal position of spouses as individuals within marriage and to recognize marriage as a form of partnership.

In my experience as a family law lawyer, this "equal position" just does not exist. Women have less money than men; women have different employment and business experience than men; women are viewed as having different needs than men.

Women go into marriage thinking it may be a "form of partnership" but often learn later on that the "form" is one of unequal partners. Like it or not, as well as being a human relationship marriage is most definitely an economic relationship. Few women find out in time what weak economic partners they really are.

I have known many women who have simply assumed that they and their husbands will share everything equally, and who only at a time of crisis have realized that this is not so. Unfortunately women have been taught that it is not nice, not romantic to consider financial questions in the context of marriage; that it is not nice or romantic to ask for what they think should be their share. That is beside the point. Husbands get their share and more, with little worry about whether it is nice or romantic. They do this every day in the business world and simply carry this ethos over to their "marriage partnership."

Not that getting their economic due from the marriage partnership will solve all of women's problems. Not until they are treated equally and *are* equal, in *every* respect, will that be possible. But at least if they view marriage as men do, as in large part an economic partnership, they will have moved one step forward.

Of course, as you will see throughout this book, this is not always possible, given the views of judges and legislators. But at the same time as women work toward changing those views they can also take advantage of what's coming to them now. Too often women simply do not know what they are entitled to during marriage or when a marriage breaks down. Either they have not been told, or they have been misinformed. Reports in the media like *New Law Gives Women Fifty/Fifty Share In Marriage Breakup* do not help, because the claim is inaccurate. But not only do women not know what they are entitled to in either marriage or divorce, they also do not know how to go about getting it.

Ironically, you find out most about the legal position of women in marriage by seeing what happens to women when marriages break down. So although this is a book intended for all women who are married or thinking about getting married, it turns out that most of what I've written is about what happens when marriages come to an end. For someone who is thinking about getting married or who is happy in her relationship now, it might seem rather odd to spend time finding out about what happens when things don't work out. In fact, though, most women find it helpful to know about marriage breakdown. It helps make them more aware of the fundamental realities of their situation, and it helps them be sure that they make decisions about their lives that protect their own interests. Certainly that's not a romantic approach to take. But, on the other hand, if a woman doesn't ensure that she is taking care of her own interests, who else is going to? And a good measure of realism isn't necessarily harmful to a relationship; in fact it may make it easier for both partners to ensure, from the beginning, that they deal with each other in the fair and equitable way most people intend.

This is not meant to be a "how-to" book. It does not tell you how to get divorced — what papers to draw up, where to sign them, how to proceed from there. It does attempt to tell you what to expect from the laws relating to marriage, separation and divorce, and how to approach these questions.

Most of the laws relating to marriage actually relate to marriage breakdown, so although the book begins with a chapter on your rights and obligations in marriage, it is quite short. Included in it is a discussion on marriage contracts. There is then a chapter on marriage breakdown, what issues you should consider when it occurs, whether and when you should hire a lawyer and how to choose one. The book then goes on to the major real issues involved in any marriage breakdown — divorce, custody, property division and support — whether you should ask for any or all of these, what you can expect given your situation and how best to make your case. Once again these chapters are not about "how to" do a divorce, but what might be expected of you, what you might have to prove in court if you want divorce or custody and what your chances might be. After these chapters comes one on separation agreements — what they are, what to include in them, and whether to sign one.

Laws relating to marriage, separation and divorce come about in two ways. First there is legislation, for example the federal Divorce Act and the provincial family law reform acts. (Quebec's laws are substantially different from those in the other provinces and territories and are *not* covered in this book.) I have tried not to be technical in referring to legislation. For the purposes of this book, it is more important that you know the overall thrust of the legislation than the specific wording or section of it.

But knowing the legislation is never enough. What you have to know is how judges have used the legislation and how they interpret it. Knowledge of both the legislation and its interpretation can often serve as a guide to how your situation will be treated in court. For example, the Divorce Act allows you to get a divorce if you have been living "separate and apart" from your husband for a certain period of time. But what if you are living as strangers in the same house? Will that suffice? You will see in chapter 3 on divorce examples of how judges have treated such situations and this may give you an insight into your own case.

Lawyers have two approaches when dealing with previous cases that interpret legislation. Depending on what they want, they may say that the case they are dealing with can be "analogized to" or "falls on all fours with" the previous case. Or they may say that the case can be "distinguished" from the previous case. If, to go back to the previous example, you have been living as a stranger in the same house as your husband for three years and want a divorce, your lawyer will ask you what your daily routine was and what contact you had with your husband. You might say, "We slept in separate bedrooms, we bought our own food, we cooked our own meals and did our own laundry." You might also say that occasionally you went to movies and a few parties together. Your lawyer will then try to find previous cases with fact situations similar to yours where a divorce was granted. He or she probably will not be able to find an exact duplicate but might find one where the judge found that in law, the parties were living "separate and apart" when the husband and wife slept in separate rooms, ate meals separately, and did separate laundries. Then you can say that that case can be analogized to or "falls on all fours" with yours and that you are therefore entitled to a divorce. In other words, if one judge granted a divorce in that case, another judge should grant one in yours. On the other hand, if your husband does not want a divorce, his lawyer will try to "distinguish" the previous case. He will say that in the previous case the husband and wife did not go out socially, and that is a major factor in your case that detracts from "living separate and apart." They will try to persuade the judge that the previous case is substantially different from yours and should not be applied, and that your divorce should be denied.

As you are reading through this book, you will probably find it helpful to use this process of legal thinking in trying to assess your own position. As illustrations are given, try to see how closely they resemble your situation, but remember they will never be exactly the same. However, are they close enough that they can be analogized and applied? Or must they be distinguished? There is of course no guaranteed answer until your case is heard, if ever, in court.

If you are interested in finding out more about the illustrations given throughout, you will find what are called "citations" with each example. I have taken all my examples from previous family law cases reported in a series of Canadian legal publications called the *Reports on Family Law.* The citations refer to the case name, volume number, page number and the province where it was decided. Thus *Lightfoot*, 11 RFL 242 Ont. means that the case was between the Lightfoots and can be found in Volume 11 of the *Reports on Family Law* (RFL) at page 242. The decision was from an Ontario judge. In cases where the parties want their identities protected, only initials are used. The *Reports on Family Law* are distributed all across Canada and include decisions from every province and territory. You should be able to find these reports in any law school library and in court house libraries.

You might find it useful to read some of these cases; you will probably find them very interesting and reassuring. You will quickly see that you are not alone in your predicament and that many women have had the same problems. The cases simply describe decisions that judges have given after a court hearing. The facts of each case are usually given first, so that you will know what the situation was and what was being disputed. Then the report will go on to consider the legal pros and cons and finally give a decision.

Although few would deny that men and women are treated differently in today's Canadian society, this is not readily apparent from a look at matrimonial laws. No matrimonial legislation on divorce, custody, property division or support is written specifically to treat women differently from men. But given that women are socially and economically in a different position from men, the *effect* of these laws is quite different for women than it is for men. And this is heightened by the views that most judges have of women, their roles and their needs.

Throughout the book I have tried to deal with issues that I have found to be of special concern to women in marriage, separation and divorce. I have tried to explain the legal positions and to highlight these with illustrations from reported cases. But this cannot be a book of do's and don'ts. The ingredients of every situation and of every couple's lives are different and so also the outcome of their cases. Family law cannot be reduced to mathematical equations. You cannot say that if there is a separated husband earning $25,000 with a wife and two children, the wife will get custody of the two children and $10,000 a year in support. There will always be other factors the judge will take into account: how long the marriage lasted; the emotional and physical makeup of the husband, wife and children; how much property and other assets the family has; why the marriage broke up. But at least this book can be a guide to what you might do to bolster your case, what elements of your situation you might pay particular attention to, what might be the final outcome. And in a more general way, the book should give you a better understanding of what the laws are relating to marriage, separation and divorce — and, in particular, how they relate to women. A little knowledge is not a dangerous thing.

1.
MARRIAGE

Most people do not think too seriously before they marry about what marriage means legally. They know that they are making some sort of commitment to the other person, but the details are rarely examined. Some people assume that marriage does nothing to their ability to function as individuals — financially or socially; others think it changes everything. The truth, in law, lies somewhere in between.

Must a wife take her husband's name?
A woman does not have to adopt her husband's name on marriage. If a woman has taken her husband's name, she can always change it back to her prior name. How and when she can do this is covered in chapter 3 on divorce, since divorce is usually when women want to revert to their prior names.

Does a wife have a right to her husband's earnings and income?
Marriage does not give a woman an automatic right to her husband's earnings and income. Nor does it give a man an automatic right to his wife's earnings and income. Each party is entitled to keep his or her earnings and income separate. A wife does have the right to be supported by her husband, although in many provinces this right is now secondary to an obligation to support herself. This means that only if she cannot support herself can a wife enforce her husband's obligation to support her. In addition, many provinces now have made the secondary obligation to support a spouse mutual — a wife can also be made to support a husband.

Although some provinces now allow this right to support to be enforced even while the spouses are still living together, in fact most cases are brought to court once the spouses have separated. The criteria for support will be dealt with in chapter 6 on support and maintenance.

Is a wife responsible for her husband's debts?

Just as the income of one does not automatically become the income of the other, so neither do the debts of one automatically become the debts of the other. The mere fact of your marriage alone does not make you responsible for your husband's bank loan. Only if you sign as a co-debtor or if you guarantee the loan can the bank come after you. If you sign nothing, you need not worry. It's a different matter, however, if you somehow do sign for a loan; you should always seek independent advice before doing that. No matter what anyone tells you, no matter how much they say, "Don't worry, we'll never come after you, this is a mere formality," once you sign you are responsible.

Is a husband responsible for his wife's debts?

Just as a wife is not responsible for her husband's debts, so a husband is not responsible for his wife's. The twist here is that often a woman cannot get credit or a loan without her husband's signature. This is changing, however, and if a woman does obtain her own credit in any form such as a loan or a charge card, her husband is not responsible if she defaults.

The only exception is if a wife pledges her husband's credit for "necessaries of life." If a wife needs food, shelter or other "necessaries of life," and can get a third party to give her these on the basis of her husband's name, the husband will then be responsible whether he signed or not. (In some provinces, this law has been expanded so that a husband can equally pledge his wife's credit.) If, however, the husband (or wife) has previously advised the third party, for example the corner grocery store, that he will not be responsible for such debts, he cannot be made to pay. And from a practical point of view such pledging of the spouse's credit is rarely accepted. Most third parties do not want to take the risk.

Does a wife become co-owner of her husband's property or business?

The simple answer is no. Spouses do get certain rights to property when a marriage breaks down, but until then the marriage itself has very little effect. Chapter 5 on property explains this more thoroughly. Never assume that because you are married, you are legally entitled to half of your husband's property or business. You may feel you should be, because of direct or indirect contributions, but the law says otherwise.

Does a wife inherit her husband's estate?

A husband can leave his estate to whomever he wishes. His wife does not have an automatic right to it. However, if a husband dies without a will, the largest chunk of the estate (what's left of his property after debts) will automatically go to his wife. Even if he has a will leaving his estate to someone else, his wife can go to court if she is in need and have a portion of the estate paid to her. How much she will get will depend, among other things, upon the size of the estate and her own needs.

Other rights and obligations in marriage

Most matrimonial laws relate to what happens on separation or divorce, which is when potential rights and obligations are turned into reality. As long as things are going well, as long as there is agreement, the law is generally not concerned with how spouses control their affairs. But knowing what the law says about your rights on marriage breakdown might help you decide whether or not to get married; whether you are getting a fair share in your marriage; and whether and when to get out of the marriage you are presently in.

What is the difference between being married and living together?

There used to be major differences between the legal implications of being married and those of living together, what people sometimes call living "common law" although the term has little legal significance. A "common-law wife" did not have the right to get financial support from her partner; now many provinces allow her to apply for it just as a married woman may. There are still limitations on when these women can actually receive support, however; this is discussed in chapter 6 on support and maintenance.

The children of non-marriage unions used to be considered illegitimate, and did not have a right to inherit any part of their father's estate when he left no will. Many provinces have now abolished the distinction between illegitimate and legitimate children, giving all children equal rights.

One major difference still exists, however, and that is in the area of property rights. Although a wife does not acquire any rights to her husband's property during a marriage, she does have certain rights when that marriage breaks down that an unmarried partner does not have.

MARRIAGE CONTRACTS: WHAT ARE THEY?

Marriage contracts are contracts or agreements made between a husband and wife before or during marriage, setting out terms concerning property division and other issues that will apply throughout the marriage and perhaps upon separation. Such contracts were once considered null and void and were not recognized by Canadian courts. Since there is usually reference in the contract to what will happen should there be a separation, they were considered to encourage the breakup of marriages, which was against public policy. But as the provinces passed their property reform legislations, discussed in chapter 5 on property, they also included provisions allowing for marriage contracts.

What do marriage contracts deal with?

Here are a few matters that you might consider putting into a marriage contract. But to understand marriage contracts thoroughly you may want to come back to this section after reading chapters 5 and 6 on property and support. Only if you are aware of what the law entitles you to in those areas will you be able to decide realistically what you want in your marriage contract. A sample marriage contract is set out in the appendix of the book to give you an idea of what they contain.

The British Columbia, Alberta, Manitoba and Saskatchewan laws allow spouses to contract out of any or all of their provisions dealing with property ownership and division. The contract may be entered into before marriage, but only takes effect upon marriage. It can deal with the ownership and division of property during marriage or on marriage breakdown. The spouses might want to agree that, notwithstanding the legislation that gives equal division of certain property if and when they separate, the property will go to whomever purchased it; or that seventy-five percent of certain property will go to the wife and twenty-five percent to the husband; or that certain property named will go to the wife and other property named will go to the husband. Basically, the parties can agree to divide their property however they wish.

In Ontario and Prince Edward Island, spouses may enter into marriage contracts before or during marriage. These contracts may deal with property division, support obligations, the education and moral training of their children and "any other matter in the settlement of their affairs." They cannot, however, deal with custody of and access to their children. That is, the spouses cannot say that either during marriage or upon separation, one or the other spouse will have custody. Nor can the contracts change the provision in the legislation that gives both spouses the right to occupy and dispose of the matrimonial home.

The Ontario and Prince Edward Island laws also allow "cohabitation agreements." These are agreements between a man and a woman who are living together but not married.

What makes a marriage contract valid?

All the provinces require that a marriage contract be in writing and signed by both parties. In Ontario, Prince Edward Island and British Columbia, the signatures must be witnessed. The requirements in Alberta and Saskatchewan are more stringent in that there must be an acknowledgment by both spouses that (a) each is aware of the nature and effect of the agreement; (b) each is aware of possible future claims to the property; and (c) each is executing the contract freely and voluntarily without any compulsion on the part of the other spouse. Finally, these acknowledgments must be made before lawyers, one for each spouse.

Why enter into a marriage contract?

Certainty. Subject to what is said below concerning a judge's power to override terms in marriage contracts, contracts do provide a measure of certainty about who will get what, should the marriage dissolve, or even while the marriage lasts. Given the wide discretionary powers the courts have concerning property division and support payments, without a marriage contract you will never be sure how property will be divided on marriage breakdown or how much support you will get.

Options. Some spouses do not want their property affected by the reform legislation. A wife may not want a cottage that she purchased herself to be divided; a husband may not want the court to give his wife a share in his non-family assets. If they can agree to opt out, regarding either some or all of their property, they may want to enter into a marriage contract.

Some couples, on the other hand, may want to divide property in a way more generous to one spouse than the legislation provides. For example, in Ontario the legislation does not guarantee a wife a share in her husband's non-family assets upon separation, so the parties might want to ensure by contract that she will receive some share.

What are the problems with marriage contracts?

The difficulty with marriage contracts is that they are usually made when all is going well and the future looks rosy. It is difficult in such circumstances to think of a marriage breakdown. But since one of the essential purposes of marriage contracts is to provide for what will happen upon marriage breakdown, their negotiation must be conducted in a realistic and business-like manner. Otherwise they should not be entered into at all. If you are giving away rights in a marriage contract that you would be entitled to under the legislation, with the assumption that the marriage will never break down, you are better advised not to enter into a marriage contract at all.

When will courts overlook the terms of marriage contracts?

Sometimes when a marriage actually ends, one spouse is dissatisfied with the marriage contract he or she signed and wants the issues decided in court. The judge will not consider the matter unless certain conditions prevail. If the formalities discussed earlier were not observed — for example, the contract was not witnessed — the contract is unenforceable and the judge may overlook it. In British Columbia, the judge may also overlook the property divisions set out in marriage contracts if he considers them "unfair" in regard to factors such as the duration of the marriage, the date the property was acquired, and "any other circumstances . . . ." In Ontario and Prince Edward Island, the judge may overlook provisions in a marriage contract relating to support obligations, if the provision or non-provision of support results in circumstances that are unconscionable, or leads to the dependant spouse requiring public assistance, or if there has been a default in payment according to the provision. If any of those three factors exist, the judge can overlook the marriage contract and make his own determination concerning support.

Usually, however, the terms of a marriage contract are binding. What you agree to now will apply in ten years or twenty, even if the circumstances have changed. So be careful before signing a marriage contract. Treat it like any other contract you sign. Know what rights you would have without the contract, what rights you are giving away, and what you are getting in return. And before signing, go over it with a lawyer.

2.
MARRIAGE BREAKDOWN

Marriage breakdowns seem to happen in stages. First there is the feeling that something is wrong, often accompanied by the hope that the problem is temporary. At this point you may try to work things out — either on your own or with the help of a marriage counsellor or other third party. Then comes an awareness that the marriage probably must end, sooner or later. Often this creates great fear and confusion about what to do, where to go, what to ask for and in general, what will happen.

Although this is inevitably a time of emotional trauma, it helps, at least from a legal point of view, if you can delineate the issues you should consider. The law, lawyers and judges are only equipped to deal with certain *issues.* If you are aware of these issues and can clarify your problems in terms of them, the resolution of your legal problems will be much simpler. It may seem that your situation is just a complicated morass, so confusing that you don't even know what questions to ask. Generally, however, the issues break down into three major categories: children, property division and financial support. To some extent, these issues overlap and tie into each other. For example, if you get custody of the children, the issue of support will be more involved than if you do not. But at least at the outset you can think of these issues separately and consider the problems — your rights, your obligations and your wishes.

One issue you will want to consider is whether in fact you really need a divorce. It is true that when a marriage is over, the first thing most people think of is a divorce. In fact, however, a divorce is just a declaration by a judge that the marriage is legally over. As you read through this book, you will see there are many other issues, such as custody and property division, that should be analyzed and understood separately. They may be dealt with on their own, or within the context of a divorce hearing if you prefer.

Often people say at the point of marriage breakdown that they want a "legal separation." But unlike marriage and divorce, which change your legal status, separation is just a factual term. If you are living apart from your husband, you are "separated." You do not need a court order, a contract or a decree, or any other legal device to confirm this fact. You may want to consider a separation agreement, a contract that some separated spouses enter into to deal with certain outstanding issues. But when you consider a separation agreement or what you want in it, you should understand what your rights and options are in the areas of custody, property division and support, dealt with in the chapters to come. That is why the chapter on separation agreements comes at the end of this book.

SEEING A LAWYER

A women is often hesitant about calling a lawyer when the breakdown of her marriage seems imminent. She thinks it will cost too much money; the lawyer will not be sympathetic to her; the lawyer will only confuse matters or worsen the situation. Or her husband has threatened that if she goes to a lawyer, she will get nothing. These are common and often legitimate fears. But if your situation is the least bit complicated, if anything being offered you by your husband seems the least bit unsatisfactory, if your husband is doing or threatening to do anything that seems the least bit unfair — then the point of marriage breakdown, even *before* you have separated, is the best time to see a lawyer. Your lawyer will be able to guide you through the separation period and tell you what your options are. Your lawyer will discuss with you, for example, whether you should move out of the house or insist that your husband move out. And your lawyer should be able to advise you against taking any action you will regret from a legal point of view later on.

This is not to say that you should put your fate in your lawyer's hands. On the contrary, if you have some clear idea of what you want (and this, of course, should be based on what you think you can get), you should present this to your lawyer and discuss the various ways of achieving it. Your lawyer will advise you whether you are being realistic and how to go about obtaining your objectives. But ultimately your lawyer must follow *your* instructions. He or she is employed by you to do what you want.

HIRING A LAWYER

Women often have a difficult time finding lawyers they can work with. They often feel — and with good reason — that most are unsympathetic to their predicament. Fortunately many cities and towns now have women's counselling services, who will suggest lawyers who have worked successfully with women in divorce work — "family law" is the term in legal jargon. Many YWCAs have legal clinics that keep a roster of such lawyers. You need not hire a lawyer who practises only family law, but with the pace of change in family law provisions you may be more comfortable with a lawyer who has a greater familiarity with the area.

Often the best way to find a lawyer is by word of mouth — ask your friends, your neighbours, your work associates. Try to get the names of a few lawyers, not just one. But remember that just because a friend was pleased with her lawyer does not necessarily mean you will be. Be wary of hiring a lawyer who has acted for your husband in his business dealings. Although that person may be perfectly honourable and trustworthy, you will probably have nagging doubts about his or her absolute interest in your case and welfare.

Do not be embarrassed about checking out a lawyer. You are not committed to a lawyer because you have gone to one interview. It is your case and you are in charge. You have as much right to be choosy with lawyers, to consider and reject them, as you have when buying a car. You are going to have to work with this person over a long period of time, telling the lawyer intimate details of your private life. If it is important for you to know what is going on in your case, do not get stuck with a lawyer who will not explain things and treats you as if you were stupid. If it is important for you to get things moving quickly, do not get stuck with a lawyer who never seems to have time for you.

You can explain to a lawyer on your first interview that you are in the process of choosing. Before the interview, ask what the charge for the consultation will be. At the first interview ask about the fees; whether there is a charge for letters and telephone calls; whether you can pay over time or must pay when the bill arrives. Ask your lawyer whether a retainer — effectively a down payment for services he or she will perform — is required, and what would be involved in using Legal Aid. Find out whether you will be sent interim or monthly bills. Often clients have no idea how much their case is costing until they get a whopping bill at the end, and that can be months or even years later.

At the end of this interview, try to find out the lawyer's initial impressions of your case — what he or she thinks will be the points of contention, what the strategy might be, where the case might end up, how long it will take. But beware of the lawyer who gives you pat and absolute answers in the first interview. Although this might be reassuring to you, the case will probably not turn out to be that easy. No lawyer can ever get a complete picture in the first interview, because so much will depend on what the other side of the story is, what your husband has to say, what your husband and his lawyer decide on as their strategy and what other facts come to light over time. Do not allow a lawyer to give you a false sense of security. In time you will gain a sense of security on your own, and a perspective on where your case is heading.

Just because you have hired one does not mean you cannot fire your lawyer. If he or she does not answer your phone calls, does not take the steps you think appropriate or takes steps you think inappropriate, you might consider firing this one and getting a new lawyer. You have the right to do this at any time. But beware of "lawyer shopping," of thinking that if only you can get the "right" lawyer, your problems will be solved. That's about as unrealistic as looking for Mr. Right. Before you look for another one, moreover, you should confront your present lawyer to explain your dissatisfactions and see whether the problems can be remedied. It is costly to switch lawyers halfway through a case. Your next lawyer would have to cover a lot of groundwork that your first lawyer already went through.

Finally, never be afraid to ask your lawyer precisely what is happening at any time. The concepts in family law are not that difficult to understand, and you, above all, have the right to know where you stand.

3.
DIVORCE

WHY DIVORCE?

Once your marriage has broken down, there are two ways of settling outstanding issues between you and your husband — by agreement or by court order. Often issues get settled along the way by agreement (for example, division of the less valuable furniture), but just as often because the more contentious issues cannot be agreed to, everything ends up for grabs. And even if the little matters can be settled, there may be some items that you and your husband cannot agree about. That's when you will have to consider going to court.

Rather than going to court on all the separate issues one at a time, it may be better to have a judge hear all the issues together. This lessens the time, money and strain involved. Although you may go to court and ask — "sue" is the legal term — for support and custody of your children, or simply for property division, it is often advantageous to sue for a divorce, thus dissolving the marriage in law at the same time. The judge who hears the divorce case has the power to deal with all of the other issues, such as custody, access, child and spousal maintenance and property division.

At this juncture, it must be pointed out that within the Canadian judicial system, divorce is a matter under federal jurisdiction. The federal Divorce Act applies all across Canada, including Quebec. Property division, however, is a matter for provincial law and therefore the law is different in every province. This is dealt with more thoroughly in chapter 5 on property, but you should know that when you are suing for divorce and asking the judge to deal with custody and support, you can also bring an application for property division and the same judge will also decide that question.

There is another reason why you might want to sue for divorce and have all the issues involved in a marriage breakdown dealt with simultaneously. Some of the grounds for divorce in Canada are still based on "fault" — for example, adultery or cruelty — when one of the two people involved is considered to be to blame. Although there are rightly many criticisms of this concept, it is often a way for the "innocent party" to present to the judge a fuller picture of the marriage. Often this is not possible if you are simply separating and suing only for support or property division, because many of the provincial laws related solely to those subjects exclude any questions of fault.

Finally, even if there are no other issues outstanding in your case, and all you want is a decree granting a divorce, you must go to court to get one.

Who can apply?

If you are the person applying for the divorce (termed the "petitioner"), you must be domiciled in Canada. Generally, you are "domiciled" in Canada if it is your intention to make a permanent home here. Before the Divorce Act, a married woman was automatically attributed with her husband's domicile. If he was domiciled in the U.S., then even if you yourself had moved to Canada and intended to make it your home, you could not acquire domicile here. The Divorce Act of 1968 has changed that and a married woman can now have her own domicile as if she were unmarried. Only the person asking for the divorce, the petitioner, must be domiciled in Canada. It doesn't matter where the other spouse is domiciled.

If you were born in Canada, this will automatically be your domicile ("domicile of origin") and you need not worry about the issue, unless you have since acquired another domicile and are now trying to re-establish domicile here.

Once you have determined that you have domicile in Canada, there is a further jurisdictional hurdle, the question of "residency." Although divorce is a federal matter, cases are actually heard by judges in the individual provinces; therefore you must determine in what province you are going to petition. To petition in a particular province, either you or your husband (termed the "respondent" if you are the petitioner) must have been "ordinarily resident" in that province for at least one year immediately preceding the date the petition is issued, that is, filed in the court office. Ordinary residence is the place where you regularly, normally, customarily live. It is not enough if you or the respondent were born and raised in that province. This is not to say that you and the respondent cannot have jobs or excursions in other provinces, but the province in which you are petitioning must be the province of ordinary residence for at least one of you. Furthermore, a person who has had ordinary residence in the province for a year prior to the date of issuing the petition must also have "actually resided" in the province for at least ten months of the ordinary residency period.

How do you apply for a divorce?

There is no such thing as divorce by agreement. You must prove that you have certain specified grounds, as set out in the Divorce Act. When petitioning for divorce, you will sign a document known as a divorce petition, which will set out all the relevant facts of your marriage and what you are asking for. A sample divorce petition is set out in the appendix to give you an idea of what it will look like. When you have signed the petition, it will be issued or filed at the court office, ready to be served upon the respondent.

How will your husband learn of the petition?

A copy of the petition must be given personally to your husband — "served" is the legal term — so that he will be aware of the request for divorce and the other items being asked for. He will then, if he wishes, be able to oppose your request and to dispute the reasons you give for the divorce. If the ground is adultery and there is someone named as the woman he committed adultery with — termed the "co-respondent" — she too must be served. If you don't know the name of the co-respondent, the judge may give an order dispensing with the addition of her name and service of the divorce petition upon her. If you do not know the whereabouts of your husband, the judge might allow for service by advertisement in a newspaper or by mailing the petition to a home where there is a possibility of its coming to his attention. These methods are called "substitutional service"; you need not prove that your husband actually received the notice. Judges will not allow substitutional service unless you set out in the form of a written statement or affidavit all the efforts you have made to find him — for example, contacting his last known employer, a motor vehicle licence search, enquiring of his friends and relatives.

Must your husband reply within a certain time?
Once the respondent has been served with a copy of your divorce petition, either personally or substitutionally, there is a time limit within which he is allowed to make his defence. This varies from province to province, and the time is generally longer if he has been served out of the province and longer still if he has been served out of the country. Although judges are fairly strict about the time limits, they do have the power to extend them. For example, in an Ontario case where the wife had been petitioned for divorce, but exceeded the time limit (in that case twenty days) for putting in her defence or answer, the judge extended the time limit, because she had wanted to ask for maintenance as part of her answer, saying: "It is most undesirable in a matrimonial cause that a wife, even though seriously in default of her pleadings, should be given no opportunity to claim permanent maintenance and to adduce evidence in support of such claim." (*MacDougall*, 8 RFL 120 Ont.) But you should not rely on such leniency. If you are served with divorce papers, see a lawyer immediately.

Once your husband is served, what can he do?
A respondent does not have to defend or answer allegations against him, in which case the divorce will be "uncontested." You will, however, still have to prove your case in court. Obviously this will be much simpler with no one disputing your allegations or requests. Or the respondent might admit the grounds for the divorce itself but dispute any or all of the other things you are requesting. For example, he might admit that there has been a three-year separation, but dispute your claim for custody. In that case, the divorce is still "contested," since there are unsettled issues that the judge must determine. Whether your husband disputes the grounds could be a tactical question, often having to do with what other items are being claimed. If, for example, you are suing for divorce on the grounds of your husband's cruelty and asking for custody of the children, it is quite likely that your husband, if he also wants custody, will deny the cruelty grounds. It would certainly lessen his chances of obtaining custody if he were to say, "Yes, it's true, I beat my wife and insulted her, but nevertheless I still want custody of the children."

Generally, if your husband disputes one item you are asking for, he will dispute the entire divorce, including the grounds. As time passes he may concede on some of the items or grounds in order to persuade you to concede on other issues. So don't be worried if your husband denies everything when the petition is served.

As well as having the opportunity of defending or answering the allegations, your husband may also cross-petition or "counterpetition" for a divorce or for what is called "corollary relief." Thus you may petition him for a divorce on the grounds of adultery, asking for custody of the children; he, in return, may counterpetition on the grounds of your cruelty, asking for custody himself. Both cases will be heard in court at the same time.

What happens before the divorce hearing?

From the time the petition is issued, your husband's lawyer and your lawyer will usually be negotiating about the various matters in an attempt at settlement. At the same time, the pre-trial proceedings will be taking place. These may involve governmental agency reports on children, interim applications to the court and what are called "discoveries."

Most provinces require that whenever there are children of divorcing parents, a report be prepared by a governmental agency on custody and access arrangements and proposals. If custody is not in dispute, these reports are very brief and often written simply on the basis of questionnaires filled out by the people involved. If there is some dispute, a more thorough investigation will take place. In either case, these reports take some time to prepare and thus delay the proceedings.

Since divorces, particularly contested ones, take a long time to reach court (partly because of the pre-trial proceedings and partly because of crowded courts), the Divorce Act has provisions whereby interim applications may be brought to court to decide certain matters between the date of the petition and the final hearing. These might deal with interim custody of children, interim access by the other parent, and interim child or spousal financial support. Interim matters are generally dealt with by written applications and statements rather than by full-fledged hearings. They take some time, since either party may be cross examined on written statements or affidavits.

Although they are meant to settle matters on a short-term basis only, pending a full court hearing that makes a final decision, in fact interim applications are crucial proceedings even in the long term. Usually on the interim application, a statement or affidavit will be presented by the other side, disputing your request for interim relief. Your lawyer will then have a chance to cross-examine that statement in detail. This is very useful in learning more about your husband's situation. And since these cross-examinations are under oath and recorded in a transcript, they may be used later in any actual divorce trial. If at that time your husband says something different from what he said on the interim cross-examination, his credibility is put in question.

Your own cross-examination can also be instructive. It helps you to prepare for the types of questions that will be asked at the final divorce hearing and gives you an idea of the gaps and weaknesses in your own case. Thus, by the time of the divorce hearing, you may be better prepared. They will also give you the first taste of what it's like to be questioned by your husband's lawyer. By the time of your trial, if it gets to that, you might be less nervous, having gone through it once.

Often a settlement between the two sides is arrived at right after the cross-examinations. At that time, the lawyers can gauge the strengths and weaknesses of their respective cases and may recommend a settlement accordingly. For example, if on the cross-examination it becomes absolutely clear that your husband has very few financial resources, your lawyer might recommend that, rather than incurring further costs and anxiety by pursuing the divorce, you settle out of court for a more realistic sum.

Sometimes the parties will settle their differences based on what the judge decides at the interim hearing; this is especially true in custody proceedings. If the wife is given interim custody and it is expected to take another year before the actual divorce and final custody matter is heard, the husband's chances of getting permanent custody are greatly diminished. Usually the longer one has a child, the more likely it is that one will be granted final custody at the end of the line. If, after the interim hearing and the court order that sets out the judge's decision, the parties agree to settle the outstanding issues, the divorce itself becomes uncontested and is heard and settled much more quickly. There will be no more pre-trial court proceedings, and uncontested divorces are often heard in special courts that deal with them very quickly. The respondent will simply withdraw his answer or counterpetition, written minutes of settlement recording the actual agreement will be drawn up and signed, and the petitioner simply goes to court to prove her grounds for getting the divorce. Often at this juncture the respondent will be much more cooperative: for example, by admitting his cruelty or at least not denying it. At this point he has agreed to everything, and so has nothing to lose by admitting the grounds. Once the grounds are proven, the minutes of settlement will be handed to the judge, who will incorporate them into the divorce decree (or "decree nisi").

Interim orders may be influential in determining the final order not just on child custody. Even in support orders requiring a husband to make regular payments to support his wife and children, it is very rare that less is awarded at the final divorce hearing than was ordered at the interim stage.

At any time before the divorce hearing, the parties may hold what are called "examinations for discovery." (The names of these examinations vary from province to province, but the intent is the same.) At an examination for discovery, your lawyer is able to ask your husband questions about all matters relevant to the divorce, and your husband answers under oath. What is said is taken down verbatim by a special reporter, and later a transcript of exactly what was said is prepared. In turn, your husband's lawyer is able to ask you questions under oath. Like interim cross-examinations, these allow you to determine the strengths and weaknesses of your husband's case, as well as to cull all the information you can about his position before going to trial. The result is that there are really very few surprises by the time you reach court. On discoveries, your lawyer may ask your husband all the details of his finances, no matter how complex. In the Gordon Lightfoot divorce case, Mr. Lightfoot did not want to answer questions on discovery about companies "owned or controlled by" him. It was his contention that these companies were separate legal entities about which he should not have to answer questions, but the judge ordered him to. (*Lightfoot,* 11 RFL 242 Ont.)

A discovery will investigate the other side's views on the history of the marriage, the history of the children's upbringing, including present and future plans, and the financial positions of the parties including employment, income and assets. Here again, the answers are under oath and transcribed for use at the trial.

Once the pre-trial matters are concluded, the appropriate court office will be notified and a date will be set when the case will be called for trial.

Grounds for divorce

To obtain a divorce, you must prove one or more of the grounds set out in the Divorce Act. The grounds are of two types: matrimonial offences or matrimonial breakdown. Matrimonial offences include such grounds as adultery, cruelty and homosexuality. Matrimonial breakdown includes such items as three- or five-year separation, gross addiction to alcohol or narcotics and non-consummation.

MATRIMONIAL OFFENCES

Adultery

Adultery is sexual intercourse with someone other than your spouse. Obviously, direct proof of this is rare. However, adultery may be proven indirectly by showing both inclination and opportunity to commit the offence. Thus, if the respondent and co-respondent are seen together at social occasions, or seen going into one or the other's residence in the evening and not departing until morning, the judge may infer that adultery has indeed taken place. (*Shaw*, 4 RFL 392 N.S.) But proof of opportunity alone is not sufficient. You must also show inclination, circumstances around the opportunity that would lead the judge to infer that adultery has taken place. For instance, where a wife hired a detective agency to follow her husband, and the detective agency reported only that her husband and a woman had spent two nights in the husband's two-bedroom apartment, the petition for divorce was dismissed. The husband claimed that they had slept in separate bedrooms, and without any other evidence as to inclination, the judge refused to infer that adultery had taken place. (*Dion,* 9 RFL 276 Sask.)

You cannot petition for a divorce on the grounds of your own adultery; you must petition on the grounds of your spouse's. However, the fact that you too have committed adultery does not prohibit you from suing for a divorce on the grounds of your spouse's adultery.

The person who is being sued on the grounds of adultery need not answer any questions either before or at the trial that might show that such adultery was committed. Such a refusal to answer might look like an indication of guilt, but judges have said that one's refusal to answer questions relating to adultery cannot be taken as evidence of having committed it.

Even if the respondent does admit adultery, the Divorce Act prohibits the judge from granting a divorce solely on the basis of the parties' admissions. (Generally, however, an admission by the *co-respondent* in court will suffice.) Thus, you will need other corroborating evidence of the adultery — statements by friends or neighbours who have seen the respondent and co-respondent together; letters written by them to each other or to a third person, declaring their feelings; hotel or motel records; a private investigator's report.

You can sue on the grounds of adultery whether it took place while you and your spouse were living together or after your separation. As long as you are still legally married, adultery can take place.

A divorce will not be granted if the matrimonial offence, be it adultery or cruelty, has been condoned or forgiven by the petitioner. The only exception is if the judge thinks the "public interest" would be better served by granting the divorce. In determining that, the judge will consider the period of separation, the circumstances of the children, and the animosity between the parties. In a case where one act of adultery had taken place four years before the divorce hearing, and that act had been condoned, the judge nonetheless granted the divorce. He indicated that there was not the "slightest chance of bringing benefit to anyone if the marriage were forced to continue," and so he found it in the public interest to grant the divorce. (*Mark,* 15 RFL 73 Ont.)

"Condonation" means full and complete forgiveness, to the point of reconciliation. Simply having sex with the respondent after learning of his adultery is not necessarily condonation. Mutual trust and confidence must have been restored.

Cruelty

Cruelty has become an increasingly frequent grounds for divorce. It is useful to know what is meant by "cruelty" and how it is proved. Women often get used to being treated in a certain way and might be comforted (in some respects) to find that this treatment is very widespread and is seen at least by the law as "cruelty." Remember no case will be exactly like yours, but maybe one will be close enough to be analogized and applied to your own.

Cruelty as it is defined legally occurs when the respondent has treated the petitioner with physical or mental cruelty of such a kind as to render intolerable the continued cohabitation of the spouses. This does not require anything in the nature of deliberate, malicious or vicious conduct, or even the intention to be cruel. It is sufficient if, by his actions alone, the offending spouse causes the other spouse to find continued cohabitation intolerable. The judge will look at the cumulative effect of the acts, but they must be grave and weighty, not trivial. Remember, however, that in the final analysis, the test is subjective: that is, how did his behaviour affect you? Its impact on you is what counts, not the effect it might have had on other women.

Generally, when you are suing on the grounds of cruelty, the particulars of that cruelty should be set out in the petition. Only then can the respondent be given a full opportunity of denying the allegations. It is often particularly difficult for women actually to articulate in detail the behaviour they have been subjected to. You should not be afraid of elaborating your husband's wrongdoing. If he treated you in a cruel manner there is no reason to protect him.

The reported cases on cruelty vary as much as relationships do. Thus, there is no stock answer as to whether a particular course of conduct will be seen as cruel. But the case histories do reflect certain types of behaviour that are widespread and treated in law as cruelty.

Rejection of the marriage. In several cases, judges have found a rejection of the marital relationship in one form or another to constitute cruelty. Where the husband left after every supper and would not return until the early hours of the next day, never went out with his wife socially and generally disregarded his wife's wishes, all of which caused the wife to become very depressed, the judge found cruelty. (*Foley,* 1 RFL 172 Ont.) Yet in a similar case, where the husband left every weekend and would not tell his wife where he was going, saying it was none of her business, the judge rejected the wife's plea of cruelty. (*Cooper,* 10 RFL 184 Ont.) In the latter case, the judge said that although there had been a marriage breakdown, there had not been cruelty. There did not seem to be any evidence of stress or depression on the wife's part. The judge said, in a rather thick-skinned manner, "It may be that the actions of the husband in staying away from home would cause a more sensitive person than this particular wife great mental distress." Here we see the subjective test at work — laced with some of the judge's perspective. Obviously, it is very important to give the judge a clear idea of the effect of your husband's behaviour on your feelings. How this is done will be discussed more fully below.

An example of the type of cruelty and its effect on a wife to which judges might be sympathetic is seen in the *Mark* case. In that case the wife was a thirty-two-year-old woman, trained as a registered nurse but not working at the time of the divorce. Her husband was a thirty-nine-year-old lawyer. When the couple married in 1962, the husband was a student in law, just about to embark on his apprenticeship as a lawyer.

Throughout the marriage, the wife, who suffered from a hereditary congenital condition that affected the connective tissues, was hospitalized on a number of occasions for various reasons, both physical and psychiatric. In fact, she had been more or less constantly under psychiatric treatments since 1967. Although joint psychiatric counselling was once recommended, it never took place.

The psychiatric reports produced at the divorce trial indicated that the wife was a hysterical personality with strong dependency needs, demonstrating strongly swinging emotions and periodic depressive reaction. The wife indicated at the trial, however, that as a result of the psychiatric treatment she had received, she now felt she was a person of some worth and dignity.

Some of the wife's allegations of cruelty were as follows:

1. For two and a half years following the marriage, her husband required her to maintain a full-time job and do all the housework. This overwork led to nervous exhaustion and hospitalization. The husband replied that this arrangement had been agreed to and that the hospitalization was due to something else.

2. The husband spent so much time working that he ignored his wife and children. He was no help with the children and his wife found it impossible to have meaningful communication with him. The husband replied that he did not work Sundays and did not ignore the children, but that he did find it difficult to engage in activities with his wife as they were not interested in the same things.

3. She claimed he was dictatorial when he did talk to her. He replied that if he had a fault, it was in not taking a *stronger* stand about things.

4. She felt unable to relate to her husband in conversation, and had the impression that her husband felt she had the intelligence of a maid. She found the nickname of "Beaver," which he gave her, an attempt to degrade her. He replied that his wife was a hard worker, that the

nickname "Beaver" was to indicate this, and that he meant it as some sort of compliment.

There were other allegations: the husband's excessive drinking; his insistence that his wife look after his large English sheep dog (in one argument, the husband allegedly proposed that the wife leave and that he would keep the dog); his unhelpfulness around the house.

The judge found that while

> virtually every one of the petitioner's allegations had some substantial foundation in fact, her version of these episodes and of the respondent's conduct amply demonstrated what the doctors, in varying terms, united in describing as a tendency to exaggerate and see the truth only in her own peculiar version.

Notwithstanding that, the judge was persuaded that the wife's view of the conduct of her husband was sufficiently close to objective reality to warrant a finding of cruelty.

The judge was particularly moved by one incident, when the wife had been hospitalized for an illness of psychiatric origin. When she was released for a weekend, her husband, instead of personally taking his wife back to the hospital, went for dinner (along with his children) to the home of a divorced woman who lived nearby. The wife was left to make her own way back or rely on her parents. The judge said, "For a woman with the dependency needs of this one to be treated in such a way demonstrates an obtuseness on the part of the respondent that is difficult to understand." The judge found that the husband's conduct caused the wife to find continued cohabitation intolerable and was thus, in law, cruel.

In several cases, judges have found rejection of the marital relationship when the husband has put his work above his wife and family. In the *Mark* case, the wife alleged that her husband worked seven days a week and most nights, seldom coming home for dinner and returning to his home very late in the evening. The husband's attitude was vividly illuminated in his testimony when he talked of "giving" his Sundays to his wife, and in references to the amount of "billable" time he had spent with his wife and children. (*Mark,* 15 RFL 73 Ont.)

Judges readily find a rejection of the marriage relationship and therefore cruelty when the husband stops communicating with his wife. In one reported case, the husband would not talk or in any way communicate with his wife for eight months. (*Cook,* 20 RFL 134 N.S.) In another, the husband not only would not talk to his wife, but followed her whenever she went out, making it difficult for her to leave the house. (*Franzen,* 22 RFL 221 Man.) However, in yet another case, the judge found lack of communication on the part of a taciturn husband (conversation in the household was nil) not to be cruelty. (*Joell,* 9 RFL 285 Man.)

Arrogant and critical behaviour. Some of the most frequent types of cruelty cases are those in which husbands adopt superior and critical attitudes toward their wives. In one case, the wife was obviously a person who craved affection and approval. The husband, however, adopted a severely critical attitude toward everything she did, undermining her self-confidence so badly that it began seriously to affect her health. The judge found cruelty. (*Farden,* 3 RFL 315 Sask.) In another typical case, a wife stated that her dominating, overbearing husband continually tried to make her think as he did, always thought he was right and wanted to subject her will to his. This made her lose confidence in herself and she became a complete nervous wreck. As she said, "I thought I should at least be free to prepare a salad as I wanted to prepare it." (*Ashraff,* 1 RFL 157 Man.) The judge gave her a divorce.

Sexual problems. Sexual matters between the parties frequently lead to allegations of cruelty. In one case where the husband repeatedly accused the wife of infidelity (an accusation the judge said was unfounded), the divorce was granted. (*Ivany,* 2 RFL 172 B.C.) A divorce was also granted where the husband persistently refused to have sexual relations with his wife. (*Delaney,* 5 RFL 44 Ont.) However, where a wife alleged that although her husband would have sex with her, he was incapable of manifesting any love or affection, to the point where sex became "utterly meaningless and excruciating," her petition was denied. The judge said this was simply "sexual maladjustment or incompatibility," but not cruelty. That case was confirmed by the Supreme Court of Canada. (*Anderson,* 8 RFL 200 S.C.C.) Where a husband refused to have children and wanted his wife's consent to his vasectomy, against her wishes, the wife was given a divorce. (*P v. P,* 7 RFL 311 N.B.)

Treatment of children. Cruelty to the wife is often reflected in the respondent's attitude and behaviour toward the children. Either the husband is critical of the wife's child-rearing ability (for example, in *Shumila,* 21 RFL 110 Man.), or he turns the children away from the mother. In one case, cruelty was found on the grounds that the husband continually denigrated the mother and indulged the children, thus frustrating her attempts to raise them in an orderly manner and casting her in an authoritarian role. (*Rowe,* 26 RFL 91 Ont.)

Physical assaults. Physical abuse is one of the most frequent cruelty allegations. Judges have held that assaults on the children are tantamount to cruelty to the wife. There have been cases, however, where an isolated assault on the wife has been insufficient for the judge to grant the divorce.

Can a husband sue for cruelty?

A husband may also sue a wife on the grounds of cruelty, but these cases are less frequent. In one case where the husband was suing because of cruelty, the judge accepted his allegations that the wife was a domineering and selfish person who made her husband feel inferior as a sexual partner; that she insisted on continuing her business career and denied her husband an opportunity of moving to another location with his company; and that she severely criticized his mother (to whom the judge found the husband to be attached "more closely than usual for males after their marriage"). But the judge denied the petition, saying that there was merely incompatibility, not cruelty. (*Hiltz,* 2 RFL 178 N.S.) However, in a number of other cases on very similar facts, judges have granted the husband's petition. In one, the husband alleged that his wife belittled and hindered him in his business activities and repeatedly referred to his "drinking problem." The judge found the wife to be "a hard, brittle, unbending, voluble person tending to dwell on trivial, irrelevant details." He found that the wife took no interest in the husband's business operations, even though he had wanted her cooperation, and that the wife's allegations of the husband's drinking problem were totally unfounded. (The husband presented evidence to support this through a doctor who had treated him for his matrimonial problems.) The judge agreed with the husband's plea of cruelty. (*Ells,* 3 RFL 353 B.C.)

In another case, the husband alleged cruelty on the part of his wife.

After he became very wealthy, his wife, in an effort to achieve her own independence and security, embarked on a course of conduct that seriously affected his physical and mental health. She embarrassed and denigrated him in remarks and in correspondence. She refused to accede to her husband's plans and wishes; she was determined to have her own way and to be "her own person," and abandoned any thought of submissiveness. She accused her husband of stinginess, even though he gave her large sums of money. The judge said that although it was not necessarily cruel for a wife to seek to achieve independence from any real or fancied domination by her husband, the means and methods employed to achieve that independence could well amount to cruelty and did in this case. (*Saxton,* 12 RFL 135 B.C.)

In another case, where a judge believed that the wife was indifferent to her husband's emotions, he found cruelty. "Mrs. Grove denied her husband sexual relations for many years, she exhibited no affection toward him and showered abuse upon him, which she heartily admits, but considers justified. She was quite indifferent to the effect of this upon her husband's enjoyment of life or mental outlook." (*Grove,* 19 RFL 128 B.C.) Where a wife developed a "close association" with another man and carried on this association near the husband's place of business, having an adverse effect on her husband's health, the husband's petition was granted. (*Chelin,* 22 RFL 254 B.C.) But where a wife associated with another man over a period of years, the judge dismissed the petition, saying her behaviour could not have made continued cohabitation intolerable, since the husband had tolerated the association for the past several years. (*Graham,* 25 RFL 107 B.C.)

How do you prove cruelty?

In 1969, guidelines were set out in the *Lacey* case that should be considered in assessing whether you will be able to prove cruelty. Although judges are not bound by these guidelines and the method of proof varies from case to case, they do highlight some elements that will be looked for. They may give you some insight into the ultimate strength or weakness of your own case.

1. Each case must be determined on its own merits. In a cruelty case, the question is whether *this* conduct by *this* man to *this* woman, or vice versa, is cruelty. In other words, the subjective test holds, as in the *Mark* case discussed earlier.

2. It is irrelevant that the conduct has caused injury to health or a reasonable apprehension of injury. The only test for cruelty defined by statute is that cruel conduct, either physical or mental, must render intolerable the continued cohabitation of the spouses.

3. In almost every case, the parties should be living separate and apart. Otherwise, a judge will suspect that cohabitation is indeed tolerable.

4. The acts complained of must be grave and weighty. "They must be insufferable, unendurable, more than flesh and blood can stand, beyond bearing."

5. The acts complained of must be more than those that merely *illustrate* the breakdown of the marriage and the incompatibility of the parties.

6. The cruelty ground must not become a way of securing a quick divorce where the evidence in respect of other grounds is imperfect.

7. The cruelty must be practised actively by the respondent against the petitioner, and not arise from the nature of things, the human condition, or the acts of third parties.

8. In general, the acts of cruelty must be corroborated.

9. In most cases, there should be an element of fear. (*Lacey,* 1 RFL 84 Ont.)

Must you be living separate and apart to prove cruelty?

Over the years, these guidelines have been commented upon and to some extent loosened. As to 3, for example, judges now realize it is often difficult for a wife to extricate herself from the family home, even though her husband is treating her with cruelty. Thus in one case, where the husband both physically and mentally abused and degraded the wife and children, the judge found cruelty and said there had been no condonation on the part of the wife, even though she had not left the home until two weeks before issuing the petition. He said that the wife had tolerated the intolerable only because her independent income was limited. Having considered the economics of establishing a new home for herself and five children, and the disorganization and disruption involved for the children (all of whom were attending school), she chose to stay in the home. This was a reasonable explanation and not inconsistent with the finding of cruelty. (*MacDonald,* 23 RFL 305 Man.) Where a wife left after an assault by her husband but then returned, the judge accepted that she had nowhere else to go and granted her petition. (*Khader,* 20 RFL 365 Ont.)

So living separate and apart from your husband is not necessarily crucial to proving cruelty or the absence of condonation. (As with adultery, a judge must dismiss a petition on the grounds of cruelty if he finds condonation, unless it is in the public interest to grant it.) If the wife has nowhere else to go, she can sometimes obtain a court order ordering the husband from the family home, in order to effect a separation. These orders are dealt with in chapter 5 on property.

A possible refuge in many towns and cities are facilities where women and children in need can stay temporarily. The police and the YWCA usually know where these interval houses or crisis centres are.

How bad does your husband's conduct have to be?

Judges have relaxed their views concerning the fourth guideline. They still expect the conduct to be "grave and weighty," but not necessarily "insufferable, unendurable, more than flesh and blood can stand, beyond bearing." Just "intolerable." Similarly, guideline 9 has been disregarded in recent cases that say explicitly that fear is not an element necessary to prove cruelty. (*Wales,* 24 RFL 138 Ont.)

Must your husband intend to hurt you?

The seventh guideline does not mean that a conscious intention by the husband to inflict cruelty is required. The judge found in the *Mark* case that there was no conscious intention on the part of the husband to inflict cruelty, but that his actions were deliberate and made continued cohabitation impossible.

What corroboration is required?

Guideline 8 calling for corroboration of evidence from other witnesses presents serious difficulties. Acts of cruelty frequently take place within the privacy of the family home, with no witnesses to the abusive conduct. Frequently a husband is a model of stability in the community but a monster at home. However, for corroboration, you do not need direct evidence of his cruel actions. Evidence such as bruises or depression will often suffice. Medical reports are frequently used in cruelty cases. It may be that the wife's physician can say that when he saw her for a particular medical problem, she seemed upset about other things and finally told him about the problems in her marriage.

The very fact that she complained about her marriage can be used as corroborating evidence in proof of cruelty. The doctor may have prescribed tranquillizers, which would be some indication of the wife's anxiety and state of mind. Or the wife might have seen a psychiatrist, before or after separation. The psychiatrist will be able to report on the wife's emotional and psychological state as a result of the marriage. And, of course, if the wife saw a doctor or attended a hospital as a result of physical abuse, the reports from these visits may be introduced.

It is useful, therefore, when leaving a marriage, to see a doctor, whether a physician, psychiatrist, or other counsellor, who will then be able to give evidence on your state of mind at that time. The stigma in court about seeing a psychiatrist is diminishing. Women used to fear that if they saw a psychiatrist or other counsellor, they would be considered crazy; that no one would believe anything they said; that they would lose custody of their children. Judges are now much more attuned to the fact that many people seek professional help before or at the breakdown of a marriage, and this can just as easily be presented as a healthy or constructive step as a negative factor.

If police were called as a result of physical abuse, their report of the incident can be used as evidence in a cruelty hearing. If a husband physically abuses his wife, she can also charge him with assault. The difficulty with this, of course, is that the woman is frequently still living in the home. A woman who fears that her husband may injure her can bring the matter to court, asking that her husband sign an undertaking to keep the peace. This is not a particularly effective protection, since only if the husband breaks the terms of the undertaking will he be punished by a fine or jail term. By then it may be too late. Both assault charges and breach-of-peace proceedings take time to reach court and by then the wife may be cajoled — mentally, physically, emotionally or economically — into withdrawing the charge. However, the mere fact that the wife laid these charges may be used as evidence in a cruelty proceeding, provided she can explain why they were not pursued. Many provinces now have legislation whereby you can obtain a "non-molestation" order against your husband. This may also be useful at a cruelty hearing.

Friends or relatives might be called to give evidence about the wife's condition while she was living with her husband. She may have been distraught, depressed, losing weight, crying a lot. Or they may have seen bruises or other evidence of physical abuse.

Remember that these are just guidelines. If you cannot see how they apply to your case, do not worry. That does not mean there is not cruelty.

Homosexual acts

A divorce may be granted if the respondent "has engaged in a homosexual act." "Homosexual act" is not, however, defined in the Divorce Act. In one case, it was found that the respondent, the wife, had engaged in a homosexual act when she engaged in kissing and petting with another woman. (*M v. M,* 7 RFL 384 P.E.I.) In another, the judge said that some actual physical act must be attested to by witnesses, that he was not prepared to infer a homosexual act by proof of opportunity and inclination alone, as would be the case in adultery. (*T v. T,* 24 RFL 57 Man.)

Other matrimonial offences

The remaining so-called matrimonial offences on the grounds of which one may petition for divorce are sodomy, bestiality, rape and going through a form of marriage with another person.

MARRIAGE BREAKDOWN

You may think that once your marriage seems to you to have broken down, you should automatically be able to get a divorce. But the Divorce Act is very strict in its definition of "marriage breakdown." A judge will find that the marriage has permanently broken down where, in addition to the husband and wife living separate and apart, certain other specified circumstances, as set out below, are proved. Only if these factors are present will a divorce be granted on the grounds of marriage breakdown.

Three or five years' separation

One of the possible specified circumstances in proving marriage breakdown is that the spouses have been living separate and apart for three years for any reason, or for five years if the person petitioning for the divorce deserted the respondent. Many petitions are brought on this ground, even where the spouses are living under the same roof. In one case, there was virtually no communication between the parties; they ate separate meals and had no social activities together. Finally, seven years before the petition, the wife left the marital bed and, apparently without protest by the husband, occupied a separate bedroom, after which there were no sexual relations between the husband and wife. The judge agreed that the spouses were living "separate and apart." (*Mayberry,* 3 RFL 395 Ont.) However, in a case where about four years before the petition, the husband moved out of the wife's bedroom and there were no further sexual relations between them, but the wife continued to do the cooking, shopping, laundry and "generally to perform duties connected with maintaining a home," the judge dismissed the wife's petition, saying that the parties had not been living separate and apart. (*Pybus,* 1 RFL 234 B.C.)

A judge will make a finding of "separate and apart" even if the spouses are living under the same roof when the following circumstances are present:

1. spouses occupying separate bedrooms;
2. absence of sexual relations;
3. little if any communication between the spouses;
4. wife performing no domestic services for the husband;
5. meals eaten separately;
6. no social activities together. (*Cooper,* 10 RFL 184 Ont.)

If the separation comes about through one spouse's deserting the other, the deserted spouse may petition for divorce in three years but the deserting spouse must wait five years. That period, however, might be shortened if in the interval the parties mutually agree that there should be a separation. At that time the separation becomes consensual, there is no longer desertion and in three years from that date, either party may petition for divorce. Moreover, the spouse who actually leaves the matrimonial home is not necessarily the deserting party. If a husband has forced his wife to leave by his attitude or actions, she may have been "constructively deserted." In that case, she has to wait only three years to petition.

The Divorce Act allows for an interruption in the three- or five-year separation if there has been a resumption of cohabitation for a single period of not more than ninety days, with reconciliation as the primary purpose. Such a trial reconciliation does not break the three-

or five-year separation. The resumption of cohabitation must be an attempt by *both* spouses at reconciliation. If only one spouse has reconciliation in mind, the period of separation will be broken. (*Pfutzenreuter,* 28 RFL 385 Man.) On the other hand, casual acts of sex during the time of separation do not necessarily interrupt the period. In one case where the spouses had had a single act of sex when they met at a friend's party, the court held that this alone did not mean there had been a restoration of the marriage state, and that this isolated act should be given no more effect in terms of ending the state of separation than in fact it had or was intended to have. (*Deslippe,* 16 RFL 38 Ont.)

Gross addiction to alcohol or narcotics

A further specified circumstance that allows a divorce on the grounds of marriage breakdown is where the respondent has been grossly addicted to alcohol or a narcotic for a period of not less than three years, and there is no reasonable expectation of his or her rehabilitation within a reasonably foreseeable period. The words "reasonable expectation of rehabilitation" imply a confident belief, for good and sufficient reasons, that rehabilitation will occur. If rehabilitative treatment has not worked in the past, then even if there is a possibility of rehabilitation at this point, it is unlikely to produce a confident belief for good and sufficient reasons that it will happen. The question of "gross addiction" is not a medical one, but rather a practical question of fact. Does the respondent indulge excessively and has he formed a dependence, physical or psychological, on alcohol or narcotics? If so, it is likely the court will find "gross addiction." (*McDonald,* 1 RFL 186 Ont.)

Non-consummation

Another specified circumstance that can show marriage breakdown is that the marriage has not been consummated *and* the respondent, for a period of not less than one year, has been unable, by reason of illness or disability, or has refused to consummate it. In one case where the wife left the husband after two months of marriage, stating quite explicitly that she was leaving him because she did not love him, could not remain married to him, and would not have sexual intercourse with him, the judge found a constructive refusal on her part to consummate the marriage sufficient to comply with the Divorce Act.

(*Knowles,* 1 RFL 251 Ont.)

Premarital sex does not constitute consummation.

Other circumstances

The remaining circumstances in which marriage breakdown will be deemed grounds for divorce are where the respondent is imprisoned for a period of two to three years, depending on the overall sentence, or where the petitioner has no knowledge or information of the respondent's whereabouts for a period of three years.

If grounds are shown, can a court refuse to grant a divorce?

When a judge finds matrimonial offences have occurred, he may not refuse to grant a divorce. However, a judge may refuse to grant a decree when marriage breakdown has been found, if it would prejudicially affect the arrangement of reasonable financial support for the children. In addition, a divorce brought under the "three- or five-years separate and apart" heading can be refused if it would be unduly hard or unjust to either spouse, or would prejudicially affect the making of such reasonable arrangements for the support of either spouse as are necessary in the circumstances. In one case, where the husband had certain war pension benefits, a portion of which was paid directly to the wife as long as the marriage was not dissolved, and where the wife was sixty years of age and unemployable, the judge granted the divorce notwithstanding the wife's objection. He said it might appear to be

> unduly harsh and possibly unjust. But, of course, she would then qualify for welfare assistance. In today's society, it is not only quite acceptable but recommended that a woman sixty years of age, without assets and without income, in poor health and practically unemployable, should receive public assistance. And when she does, her situation will not be harsh or unjust. (*Bigelow,* 4 RFL 388 Man.)

This is not a very reassuring decision.

When do you get your final divorce decree?

When the case eventually comes to court and the divorce is granted, the petitioner will be granted what is termed a "decree nisi." If within three months the spouses have not reconciled, or no appeal has been launched, this decree will be made absolute, or final, upon the filing in court of certain papers. You need not attend court for this. On some occasions, the divorce court will shorten the three-month period, even making the divorce final at the divorce hearing. This may occur if the judge considers that by reason of special circumstances it would be in the public interest to do so *and* if all the parties undertake not to appeal. Often the judge will consider it in the public interest to shorten the time if one of the parties indicates that he or she wishes to remarry as quickly as possible because of the impending birth of a child.

What name can a married or divorced woman use?

Women may retain their maiden names upon marriage. Often, however, women adopt their husbands' names and then wish to revert to the names they used before, either during the marriage, upon separation or upon divorce. They may also wish to change their children's names to conform with theirs. The laws on name change vary from province to province, but generally, notwithstanding any legal procedures, they are free to use any name they choose.

Usually a woman may use or revert to any name without going through the formalities of a change-of-name application. A difficulty is often encountered, however, in that many government bureaucracies, for example motor vehicle offices, will not recognize a woman's name change unless sanctioned by legislation or formally changed by a court. Several provincial statutes specifically permit a married, separated or divorced woman to keep or revert to her pre-marriage surname without formality.

Basically the law is as stated by a Nova Scotia court:

> There is nothing to prevent the applicant (a separated, but not divorced woman) from using her maiden name and indeed, any name or surname that she can persuade her friends and acquaintances and the public in general to call her by. . . . A name is merely a means of identification and any other name that identifies the individual in question may be used, if this is not done to defraud. (*Dillon,* 21 RFL 384 N.S.)

That judge went on to express grave doubts about public agencies who refuse to change the applicant's surname of record when the reversion to this surname has not been formalized by court order.

Almost all the provinces provide for an application to change children's names upon divorce. Usually they allow the mother, if she has custody, to apply for a change of the children's surname to her own, provided she has the consent of the father. If the children are over a certain age (usually 12 or 14), they must also consent to the change themselves. In addition, if the woman has remarried and wishes to change the children's surname to that of her new husband, the new husband must consent to the name change. In one case, a woman had remarried, adopted her new husband's name and registered the children in school under that new name, all without a formal court order, and in fact without the consent of the children's father. The father applied for an injunction, asking the court to prohibit the mother from having the children use her new surname. The judge found that the adoption of the new surname by the older children (ages 11 and 9) was their own decision, and felt that the youngest child would, in time, want to have the same surname as her sisters. The judge then decided that it was in the best interests of the children to leave matters the way they were and dismissed the father's application. (*Hoodekoff,* 25 RFL 8 B.C.)

Who pays for the divorce?

There are two types of costs to consider in matrimonial litigation — those fees and disbursements you will have to pay your own lawyer and those costs that a judge might make the losing side pay to the winner. Even if you get court-awarded costs, they will not usually cover all the fees and disbursements you will have to pay your own lawyer. Court-awarded costs are based on a provincial tariff for court costs, and this tariff is often lower than what lawyers charge their clients directly. Thus, one is rarely fully reimbursed even if the other side has to pay your costs.

The general rule used to be that in matrimonial matters, costs were awarded to the wife, even though she might be unsuccessful in the application. This has changed; it is simply a matter of judicial discretion who, if anyone, will be awarded costs. Wives are no longer in a preferred position. Some judges have said that when a divorce is based on marriage breakdown, and there is no fault on either side, no costs should be awarded. Often judges will consider the conduct of the parties during the proceedings in determining an award of costs. In one case where the husband had used delaying tactics in disclosing financial information, the judge awarded costs to the wife, noting that the husband had been responsible for the protracted nature of the proceedings, which resulted in substantial fees and disbursements for her. The judge also noted that the husband was far wealthier than the wife and therefore in a better position to bear the costs. (*Anderson,* 19 RFL 344 N.B.)

Similarly, where the wife did not work during the marriage, at the husband's request, and did not acquire any assets, the judge first noted that a wife should not get costs merely because she is a wife, but went on to say that these particular facts favoured awarding her costs. (*Lazenby,* 18 RFL 393 B.C.)

Increasingly, judges look at pre-trial offers of settlement to determine whether there should be an award of costs. In one case where the husband had made a more substantial offer of settlement than the wife actually got at trial, the judge did not award her costs, even though she had won her case. He noted that she could have lessened the time and money spent had she accepted the husband's pre-trial offer. (*Cameron,* 3 RFL 2nd 277 Ont.) These trends in decisions put a heavier onus on spouses to consider seriously the other side's pre-trial offers; they may not have costs ordered in their favour if they decline an offer of settlement that is higher than the court order, and may even have costs awarded against them.

Just as costs used to be awarded automatically to wives, so also they used to be awarded against male co-respondents in adultery actions. This, too, has changed. It has become entirely a matter of judicial discretion whether a male co-respondent will be ordered to pay the husband's costs in an adultery action. In one case where the judge was satisfied that the co-respondent actually had nothing to do with and was not responsible for breaking up the marriage, in that it had failed irreparably before the adultery, he refused to order costs. (*McKay,* 19 RFL 32 B.C.)

4.
CHILD CUSTODY AND ACCESS

Some of the most bitter battles upon separation or divorce are about custody of the children. It is very difficult to separate your animosity for your spouse as a mate from your view of that spouse as a parent. But if the parents cannot agree who will have custody of the children, it is left to the courts to decide. This might be done in the context of a divorce proceeding (and here any cruelty allegations will certainly colour the judge's view of who should have custody) or on its own, if you don't have grounds for a divorce or don't want one at this juncture. All the provinces have legislation that allows a custody application to be brought on its own.

A court will rarely interfere with parents' private agreements concerning custody. You can agree to any of the custody or access arrangements discussed in this chapter. Only if you *cannot* agree must you go to court.

What does custody mean?
When one spouse is granted sole custody of a child, that party is inherently vested with the sole right and sole responsibility for the child's care, upbringing and education, including religious instruction.

What are the age limits in custody matters?
Just as with a petition for divorce, there are preliminary matters to be considered before you can bring a custody application. The first one is the age of the child or children. If you are bringing the custody application in the context of a divorce action, the Divorce Act limits the right of the judge to determine custody. A child must be under sixteen years of age, or if over sixteen years of age must be unable, by reason of illness, disability or other cause, to withdraw himself from his parents' charge or to provide himself with the necessaries of life.

Several custody cases have been heard where the child was even twenty or twenty-one years of age, but still at school. If the custody application is made under the terms of provincial statute rather than the Divorce Act, the statute itself will set a limit — usually age seventeen or eighteen — beyond which the judge does not have jurisdiction.

Judges are often hesitant to make custody orders in relation to children fifteen years of age or older, since they recognize that at that point the children can simply make their own choice, and the courts cannot supervise these custody orders with any degree of effectiveness. If they do make custody orders in relation to children in that age group, judges will give the greatest weight to the children's wishes. (This is discussed in more detail below.)

In which province should custody be sought?

The second preliminary matter is determining in what province to bring the custody application. Generally, only the court in the province where the child is ordinarily resident will determine a custody matter. A child is considered to be resident in the province where he is dwelling with permanence or for a considerable period of time. This cannot be changed by a parent's simply removing the child to another province. For example, if a divorce case has started in New Brunswick and then one spouse moved with the children to British Columbia, the New Brunswick court will still make the custody order. That court has jurisdiction over the children ordinarily resident in its province, even though they may be temporarily outside it. (*Adams,* 7 RFL 203 N.B.) In one case, where a father brought children to Ontario while custody proceedings were going on in England, the Ontario judge would not make a custody order, the children not being resident in that province. In fact, the judge ordered the children returned to England. (*Loughran,* 9 RFL 255 Ont.)

On the other hand, a judge may make a "protective custody" order even if the children are not ordinarily resident in his province. This might happen if the judge is convinced that the applicant has taken the children from the province of ordinary residence to protect their welfare. Even then, however, the judge will probably order the permanent custody hearing to be in the province of ordinary residence. (*Cochrane,* 20 RFL 264 Ont.) Even though protective custody is possible, you should be very careful about taking your children and moving to another province. The children may be ordered returned.

Who has custody of the children before the final trial?

Like divorce cases, custody disputes take some time to reach court. In those circumstances, there is usually an application for "interim" custody, to decide who will have legal custody in the interval. This will probably be done by written application and affidavit. The parties might also file affidavits of other witnesses; there may be cross-examinations on all of these affidavits. Unless this material is extremely impressive, interim custody is given in most cases to whichever parent has had *de facto* or actual physical custody since separation. It is very important, therefore, that you not give up physical custody of the children if you are intending to pursue legal custody. The judge will not disturb the *de facto* situation unless there are very compelling reasons to do so. And the judge will look at the *original* situation — he will not allow a parent who snatches a child at some point after separation to claim *de facto* custody. (*Sobanski,* 9 RFL 318 Ont.)

As indicated in chapter 3 on divorce, settlement is often reached after cross-examinations on the interim custody application. This might be because of detrimental facts that came out on either party's cross-examination. For example, the father might admit under cross-examination that he really does not know much about his children's routine, and in fact has no concrete plans for their future. And even more often, a settlement is reached after an order is issued for interim custody. This is largely because of the difficulty of winning a final custody case if you do not have interim custody. Judges seem very hesitant to move children from the home they are in at the time of the trial, unless the current situation is obviously detrimental to them or the move would clearly be in their best interests.

It is rather difficult to develop a case for custody if you do not have the children residing with you. If your husband has the children, he can obtain school reports saying the children are doing well, academically and socially; doctors' reports saying the children are healthy and well adjusted; neighbours' reports saying the children are happy and well behaved; visitors' reports saying the household is clean and well maintained. Naturally there are ways of attacking the interim custodial parent's behaviour and of bolstering your own case, but the battle is much tougher.

How is final custody determined?

In determining custody, it is now a fixed principle that the best interests of the child are the paramount consideration. Other factors should only be considered if they affect the child's best interests. For example, the mother's adultery should not be considered in and of itself, but only as it affects the best interests of the child.

Some provincial statutes give the judge guidelines on what to consider in determining custody, while others such as Ontario's and Prince Edward Island's simply say that the judge shall order custody in accordance with "the best interests of the child." The Divorce Act tells the judge to do what he thinks is "fit and just," having regard to the conduct of the parties and the condition, means and other circumstances of each of them.

The British Columbia family law reform act is very explicit about what the judge shall consider in determining custody. It states that the best interests of the child are paramount, and in assessing these interests, the judge shall consider:

1. the health and emotional well-being of the child, including any special needs for care or treatment;
2. where appropriate, the views of the child;
3. the love, affection and similar ties that exist between the child and other persons;
4. education and training for the child;
5. the capacity of each person to whom guardianship, custody or access rights and duties may be granted to exercise those rights and duties adequately.

The Saskatchewan Infants Act has similar directive guidelines saying that the welfare of the child is the only relevant consideration, and that in determining the child's welfare, the judge is to consider the physical, psychological, social and economic needs of the infant. It goes on to direct the judge to take into account certain factors similar to those set out in the British Columbia act.

WHAT EVIDENCE WILL BE USED AT THE CUSTODY TRIAL?

The child's wishes

Often judges will interview older children to see where they want to live. As noted previously, judges recognize the difficulties in making a custody order against the wishes of an older child. Usually the judge will interview the children privately, with or without lawyers but invariably without the parents present. It is difficult to say at what age a child is considered old enough to have his or her wishes considered, but at least one judge remarked that the views of a six-year-old are not relevant. (*Knowles,* 2 RFL 2nd 396)

A recent innovation in custody cases is having children represented by their own lawyers. Your lawyer can give you an idea of how the judges in your area or province have taken to this development, should you wish to consider it for your case.

There is a difference between interviewing a child about his or her wishes concerning custody and calling the child at a custody hearing to give evidence about the circumstances, such as a parent's conduct. Judges tend to disapprove of having children give evidence.

Home study reports

Frequently a judge will consider or ask for a report of the appropriate governmental agency involved with children's welfare. These reports will be based on interviews with the parties involved, house visits and perhaps interviews with other witnesses, such as teachers. Sometimes the reports will set out the facts in as neutral a fashion as possible; at other times they will implicitly or explicitly favour one party over the other. Because of their official veneer and apparent impartiality, they are given considerable weight. You should be as cooperative as possible in filling out these reports, because what you say will become part of the record.

Psychiatric and psychological reports

Increasingly, one or both parents will introduce evidence from psychiatrists or psychologists as to their emotional and psychological suitability to raise children. This is particularly true when one of the parties is accused of being psychologically unfit. Not only will such reports be filed in court, but the psychiatrist or psychologist will also be called at the trial to elaborate upon them.

These reports are particularly important if the person asking for custody is leading what the judge might consider an unconventional lifestyle. In that case, the applicant will want an expert to advise the judge that this lifestyle will not affect the children's well-being. In one striking case, a mother who was living in a homosexual relationship called four outside witnesses to testify on her behalf. One of these had interviewed the partner of the mother and described her as "intelligent and level-headed." Another, a psychologist, had interviewed the mother, and indicated that she had "scored high in the area of self-regard." This witness had also observed the mother and child together and noticed a "close relationship between the mother and child," claiming this to be one of the best mother/child interactions she had seen in her professional practice. The child appeared to be happy and well adjusted, and an interview with her teacher confirmed this. This expert also related in her evidence some recent research on homosexuality and advised the judge that homosexual women are no more neurotic than female heterosexuals, and that homosexuality is not a disease capable of correction, nor should one attempt to correct it. The psychologist advised the judge that the manner in which one fulfills one's sexual needs does not relate to the ability to be a good parent, and that homosexuality is much more common than once thought. A third expert examined the mother and found her to be "alert, pleasant, with no major problems," and "vitally concerned for the welfare of her daughter." The fourth witness indicated that she had lived with a woman for the past five years and had custody of her daughter. She advised the judge that her own daughter was normal and well adjusted. The mother obtained custody, but probably would not have done so without the assistance of these expert witnesses. (*K v. K,* 23 RFL 58 Alta.) Expert evidence should almost always be obtained in these cases. It may be more difficult for people in small towns or communities to call on these resources, but contact can be made with professionals in larger communities and examinations arranged.

On some occasions, the parties do not want the names of their psychiatrists known, and do not want them called as witnesses. In custody cases, however, it is difficult to prevent this if the other side insists. In one case where a wife refused to disclose the name of a psychiatrist who had treated her some years earlier, the judge ordered her to do so. He said that, since ultimately the best interests of the children were at stake, the fullest possible disclosure of all facts should be made. (*Ansley,* 12 RFL 93 B.C.) If you know you are going to get an unfavourable report from one psychiatrist, try to find another psychiatrist or psychologist who will give you a favourable one, which will at least neutralize the first report.

Sometimes the parties will consent to a joint psychiatric examination of themselves and their children. Whether you will agree to this will depend on what you think the outcome will be. But it might look bad if you do not.

Either or both parties will often arrange to have the children examined by a child psychiatrist or psychologist. The interim custodial parent will do this to show the children are well adjusted and have a close relationship with that parent. The other party will do this to show the opposite. It may be difficult for the non-custodial parent to arrange for these examinations if the custodial parent does not agree to them, but they might be done surreptitiously or during visiting times.

School and pediatric reports

School reports should be introduced to show how the children are doing, both academically and socially. The custodial parent will want to introduce these if the children are doing well; the non-custodial parent if the opposite is the case. In addition, reports from the children's doctors might be introduced to attest to the children's health or lack of it.

Neighbours, friends and sundry witnesses

Since the point of a custody application is to determine what is in the "best interests of the children," both parties will want to call witnesses as to the children's general well-being at home and in the community. These witnesses may be neighbours, friends, relatives, religious or social leaders, and others who have had contact with the children. They might also attest to the parent's bonds with the children.

As noted earlier, it is much easier for the interim custodial parent to collect these witnesses by parading people through his or her home, taking children to activities and generally keeping in contact with potential allies. The non-custodial parent will have to rely on people from the past who saw him or her with the children, or on spies from the present who can say that the children are not doing so well under the custodial parent's care. The non-custodial parent must also develop contacts with potential witnesses during access periods. Instead of taking the child to the zoo on your visits, you might consider taking him or her to some activity such as gym class or music lessons, where you will find potential witnesses as to your relationship with the child.

WHAT WILL THE JUDGE CONSIDER IN DECIDING CUSTODY?

In addition to the items set out in the British Columbia and Saskatchewan statutes, there are several factors judges frequently consider in determining custody.

Who left the family home?

"Custody is not an order made by way of compensation to a parent whose spouse left him to seek happiness elsewhere, or denied by way of retribution to a parent who breaks the continuity of the marriage." Encouraging words from a judge who awarded custody to a mother who crept out of the house one night and moved with her children to another town. The judge found the children had adjusted well to their new surroundings, including the mother's new common-law relationship. The children had new friends, their teachers saw them as happy children, they were involved in many extracurricular activities, including 4-H and peewee hockey, they attended church regularly, and were in excellent health. The mother presented an ideal picture and the judge was not willing to deny her custody simply because she had left the family home. (*Tiller,* 20 RFL 79 Man.)

Sometimes mothers leave without the children. One judge said:

> The mere fact that a mother leaves her children in the custody of her husband should not of itself count against her when considering whether she should have custody of her children. In some instances, and this appears to be one of those cases, one can deduce from the conduct of the mother that she was indeed thinking of what was in the best interests of her children.

In this case, the mother had no money and nowhere to go, except to a male friend's home. She did not feel it would be in the best interests of the children to uproot them at that time. She subsequently developed a common-law relationship with her male friend and was looking after his two small children. The judge believed that she was a good housekeeper and a good mother to her male friend's children, and that this friend was honest and forthright. He did not believe, as alleged by the father, that the wife had a vicious temper and frequently hit her children. He also found that the children were happy with the mother on her interim access visits. In addition, he was impressed by the fact that the mother would be looking after the children directly, whereas the father would be employing a babysitter. The mother was given custody. (*Laberge,* 16 RFL 60 B.C.)

But in many cases, judges have been much harsher and have viewed the mother's leaving the home, with or without the children, as indicating something negative about her character. For example, one mother, having lost all affection for her husband, developed a relationship with another man. She then left the family home with her children to live with the other man. The judge ordered custody to the husband, saying:

> A parent who broke up the family home without good cause, and I do not consider the [mother's] reasons as being a good cause, is obviously not as well equipped to have the custody of the children of the marriage as her spouse, who is still desirous of re-establishing the family as a unit. This action shows a lack of character under the circumstances. . . . In my opinion, a parent who, under the circumstances shown by the evidence in this case, causes the separation of husband and wife, is more concerned about herself than she is concerned about the welfare and happiness of her children. (*Schulz,* 14 RFL 237 Man.)

Another mother left the children with their father during a trial separation of eight months. She was denied custody. The judge felt that her "abandoning" the children to the father while she went into this "prolonged state of self-examination, freed from the responsibility of the children," suggested that in a time of domestic or emotional stress or crisis, the mother would place her own interest above that of her children. The judge conceded that the father had not always been a concerned and caring father, and that his drive for personal and professional advancement had superseded his sense of responsibility toward his wife and children. He also conceded that the father's drive had been a large contributing factor to the family breakdown. But he seemed more willing to forget the father's past "selfish" conduct than the mother's. (*Bolton,* 26 RFL 284 P.E.I.)

Leaving the family home is one of the most important decisions you will have to make, particularly in its effect on custody. Try, if at all possible, to discuss this action with a lawyer beforehand. It will have grave implications.

Past conduct of parents

When examining a parent's conduct before separation, judges say they are doing this not with a view toward ascertaining blame, to then use custody as a reward or punishment, but simply to obtain some insight into the person's character and sense of responsibility. For example, if they find previous neglect of parental duties, they may deny that person custody.

A judge will be impressed by the fact that the applicant had exercised the chief responsibility for raising the children prior to separation. Where the father had been a surveyor and away from home much of the time, the judge, in awarding custody to the mother, noted that she had had the chief responsibility for raising the children. As well, she had been an "excellent housekeeper." (*Robb,* 2 RFL 2nd 172 N.S.)

That same judge remarked, in another case, that the fact that the mother was a very poor housekeeper would not be enough to divest her of custody. Her husband had neither complained nor helped while they were living together, and there was no evidence that the child had suffered in any way, physically or mentally, as a result of the messy house. (*MacKinnon,* 4 RFL 61 N.S.)

One judge was negatively influenced by the frequent affaires a mother had had while living with her husband. He felt that these acts of adultery, which allegedly broke up the family home, showed that she did not have all the attributes of a "good mother," one of which would be providing a home for *both* the parents and children. (*Bowyer,* 27 RFL 131 Sask.)

There is nothing much you can do about "prior" activities, be it child-care responsibilities or extramarital affaires. But at least you can stress your positive points and the other parent's negative points. In no other area is the mud-slinging as fierce as in custody fights. You will have to be prepared for this.

How much money does each parent have?

In principle, judges reject the finances of either party as a consideration in deciding custody. In practice, this is not always so. In one case where the mother was a waitress and earning an income below the poverty level, without even enough money to pay a babysitter, custody was given to the father. (*Goupil,* 9 RFL 87 N.B.)

In another, where the mother would have needed substantial financial support from her husband, she was denied custody. The judge found that the husband's salary was too low to provide support to his wife and child. But since the father was residing with his parents, who had enough money to provide for the child, he was awarded custody.

(*Banks,* 2 RFL 2nd 179 Alta.)

Age of children
Custody of young children, below the age of seven years, used to be given almost automatically to their mothers. But young children are now given to their fathers more frequently. There are, however, some cases that suggest that where the mother and father are equally good parents, young children should go with the mother.

Sex of children
Views have changed since 1955, when one judge said:

> Instinctively, a little child, particularly a little girl, turns to her mother in her troubles, her doubts and her fears. In that respect nature seems to assert itself. The feminine touch means so much to a little girl; the frills and the flounces and the ribbons in the matter of dress; the whispered consultations and confidences on matters which, to the child's mind, should only be discussed with Mother; the tender care, and the soothing voice. . . .

But even recently, one judge observed that it "must be an unusual and compelling case for a court to conclude that custody of an infant female child should be granted to the father rather than the mother." (However, in that case, custody was granted to the father because of other factors.) (*Bryant,* 4 RFL 2nd 210 B.C.)

Present conduct and living arrangements of parents
Present living arrangements are one of the major factors in any judge's determination. They indicate in what circumstances the child will be living, now and in the future. It is therefore useful to examine how judges have treated some arrangements of increasingly common experience:

Homosexuality. There have not been many cases reported that indicate what view a judge will take of a homosexual relationship. In one case where the mother was living in a homosexual relationship, the judge said that in itself should not prevent her from obtaining custody. He then went on and awarded custody to the father, who he said was "stable, secure and responsible." (The father's hobby was shooting rifles and handguns, and he had quite a collection of firearms in his house. The judge felt, however, that he was responsible with these weapons.) In contrast, the judge found the mother's way of life to be "irregular." At one point, the judge said he was especially concerned about placing the children with the mother since he had not heard testimony from the woman with whom the mother was living. Therefore he did not have enough information about the situation in which the children would be placed. He went on to say, however, that there was "another factor." That factor was his fear "that if these children are raised by the mother, they will be too much in contact with people of abnormal tastes and proclivities." It was probably more than just "another" factor. (*Case,* 19 RFL 132 Sask.)

A more encouraging case for those living in homosexual relationships is one decided in an Alberta court. In that case, the "other woman" was called as a witness and the judge was very impresssed with her. He was also impressed by the "discreet" manner in which the women carried on their relationship — "not flaunted to the children or community at large." He distinguished the *Case* judgment referred to above because in that instance, the mother had been active in a homosexual association and was an officer of a homosexual club that often met at her home, whereas in the case before him he found the mother not to be a "missionary" about homosexuality. (*K v. K,* 23 RFL 58 Alta.)

Lifestyle. Judges are rather suspect if there is a radical change in the lifestyle in which the applicant for custody is presently living, as opposed to what the children were used to when the family lived together. In one case where a mother had left a rural, well-disciplined and Catholic environment to move to the city, where she lived in an apartment and was frequently visited by her boyfriend, the judge denied her custody. He stated that although he was perhaps old-fashioned, he felt that introducing the children to an "immoral atmosphere" contrary to the religious teachings of the church to which they belonged left much to be desired. He felt the children would be better off returned to their father, who would provide them with continuing development in the same environment and same religious atmosphere. (*Skbovius,* 1 RFL 2nd 284 Man.) In another case, where a mother left home and joined a sect that believed in communal parenting, the children were also returned to the father. (*Robichaud,* 6 RFL 2nd 232 Sask.)

Cohabitation. Many judges have said that a mother's new non-marriage relationship does not affect the question of custody. Several have even applauded such moves, stating that in a new and better relationship, the woman would be a better mother to her children than she was before. (*Laberge,* 16 RFL 60 B.C.) Judges are especially easily persuaded if they like the new partner and the relationship appears stable.

In fact, some judges are so enthusiastic about these relationships that a "single" parent can be at a disadvantage. In one case where the mother intended to remain single but the father intended to marry the woman with whom he was living, the judge gave custody to him. He said both parents were capable of providing a good and loving home, but that "the chances of successfully raising children are enhanced by a two-parent family." (*Miller,* 27 RFL 189 B.C.)

There are still traditional judges, however, who are reluctant to expose children to a non-marriage relationship. One judge who in the end gave custody to the mother, even though she was living in such a relationship, could not resist noting his disapproval of the situation, "despite the publicity given to similar establishments amongst leading celebrities in the theatrical and movie world." (*Greenhow,* 9 RFL 95 Sask.)

Religion and race. Judges generally say that they will not give weight to matters of religion other than a general consideration of its effect on the well-being of the children. In one case, a father had become a Buddhist and at one point was operating a Darma centre, where he and the children had lived. The mother said she wanted the children brought up in the Christian faith. The judge concluded that there was merely a difference in the parties' philosophical outlooks, and that there was no particular advantage in either of them relative to the welfare of the children, save that the father's situation seemed more settled and permanent than that of the mother, who had only recently returned to an exploration of the Christian religion. The judge gave the father custody. (*Henderson,* 29 RFL 1 B.C.)

One judge who gave custody to a mother who had become a devout Jehovah's Witness, did so only on the condition that should any of the children require medical services, the right to give any necessary consent for medical procedures would be vested in the father. (*Robb,* 2 RFL 2nd 172 N.S.)

It is difficult to say how significant a factor race might be in determining custody in mixed marriages. In a case involving a child of a Sikh father and a Canadian-Irish mother, the judge considered the race of the father highly significant. He gave custody to the father, stating:

> This boy is a Sikh; he will always be regarded as a Sikh in this country. It will be well for him to be brought up as a Sikh, to preserve the existing knowledge of the Punjabi language, to be schooled in the religion and traditions of the people with whom he will always be associated. It will, in my view, be possible for him to find a secure personal identity only in the Sikh community. It is the only identity our society will permit him. Let him, then, be a Sikh and be proud of the tradition and accomplishments of a proud and worthy race. No matter how much she loves him, his mother cannot accomplish this. (*Hayre,* 11 RFL 188 B.C.)

Future plans. One of the most crucial points in custody hearings is the presentation of future plans in relation to finances, residence, child care and any other matters that might affect the child. Obviously a judge will want to know in what sort of environment he is placing the child. If you come to court with concrete plans, the judge is more likely to believe you are taking the responsibility of custody seriously. This is especially true if you are no longer living in the family home. The parent residing in the family home has an almost ready-made case regarding residence, schooling, and extracurricular activities.

It is therefore incumbent upon the parent outside the home to present an equally concrete plan for the children. It is often very difficult for women who have left the family home to do this. They may not have jobs, or only ones that are poorly paid. There will be problems, then, in committing themselves to large expenses for accommodation and other provisions before they know whether they will have custody and child support. But they can at least investigate the possibilities in their new communities and go to court with some plans of where they intend to live, how much this will cost, and what the educational and other facilities in the area are.

Sometimes a mother's work plans will be held against her. If she proposes to place the child in daycare, she will have to convince the judge that the service will provide the same emotional and physical benefits to the child as any babysitter the father might hire.

TYPES OF CUSTODY ORDERS

Separation of siblings

Judges are hesitant about interfering with sibling relationships, but there are cases where they will divide the custody so that one or more of the children go with one parent and the remaining ones with the other.

Divided custody

Occasionally, judges will make orders of divided custody — putting the children under the custody of one parent for part of the year and of the other parent for the remainder. In one instance where the judge felt there was little difference between the merits of the parents, but also was of the opinion that the mother should play the dominant role, he divided custody, giving the children to the mother from January to June and September to December of each year, and to the father for July and August. In that case, the mother lived in Ontario and the father lived in Saskatchewan. If they had lived in the same province, the judge probably would have simply given custody to the mother and access to the father during July and August. (*Buchko,* 11 RFL 242 Sask.)

Joint custody

A current trend among separating parents is to allow for joint custody arrangements. Effectively both parents retain custody and the rights and obligations attached thereto, with the children actually residing with one or the other when and as the parents determine. Joint custody is regarded by judges as an exceptional disposition reserved for a limited category of separated parents. There must be a high degree of cooperation and agreement about childraising practices. The two must be willing and able to cooperate as loving parents. These exceptional circumstances are rarely, if ever, present in cases of disputed custody. Thus joint custody is usually arrived at by consent, and is rarely ordered by judges.

Unmarried parents

In the past, a mother of a child born out of wedlock had the right to custody of that child *prima facie,* unless she was shown to be "unfit." This is not true any more; as with all children, most judges will consider only what is in the best interests of the child.

Custody to people other than parents

Judges can award custody to a person other than one of the parents. There are numerous cases where custody has been granted to the grandparents. In one case where there was a three-way fight between the mother, father and maternal grandparents, custody was granted to the maternal grandparents. The child was already in their care, and the judge felt it was best to leave him there. (*Humphreys,* 4 RFL 64 N.S.)

Kidnapping

Custodial parents are often worried that the other parent will take the child out of the country and beyond the jurisdiction of the Canadian courts. One measure of prevention is to have the court order that the child's passport (if for any reason the non-custodial parent has it) be placed with a lawyer or with the custodial parent. Another possibility is to include in the order a clause forbidding one or both of the parents to remove the child from Canada without consent in writing of the other. Often the only remedy when the child is taken out of the country illegally is to retain an investigator to trace the child, pick up and return him or her. The non-custodial parent is clearly in contempt of court if he deprives the custodial parent of custody, whether it be out of the country or not, and may be imprisoned for such an action. There have been cases where the non-custodial parent has hidden the child and the judge has imprisoned that parent until he or she arranges for the child's return.

The British Columbia family law reform act explicitly makes it an offence under the act to deprive a custodial parent of custody, and the wrongdoer may be dealt with accordingly. In addition, in some cases the kidnapping parent can be charged under the Criminal Code.

Arbitration

Sometimes parties avoid court by choosing an arbitrator to decide the issues of custody and access. The arbitrator is often a lawyer or someone knowledgeable in child-care matters. This course is often more informal and less expensive than the courts. The arbitrator will use the same criteria as a judge would use, unless specifically directed otherwise by the parties.

Can a custody order be changed?

Since custody orders are made in the best interests of the child, they are never final. If the other parent believes that it is no longer in the best interests of the child to remain with the legal custodial parent, he or she may bring an application to court to have the custody order changed — the legal term is "varied." There must, however, be a material change in the conditions and circumstances. Judges will not vary the previous order lightly. They will not look for errors in the original custody order itself, but simply at how the conditions or circumstances have changed since that date to see whether a variation should be made.

ACCESS

The parent who does not have custody usually has access — visiting rights with the child. Since the parent who has custody has the primary responsibility for the care and welfare of the child, the other parent should respect the wishes of the custodial parent concerning the child's care during access periods. For example, if the custodial parent indicates that the child has a cold and is not to go swimming, or is to take certain medication, the visiting parent is under some onus to comply. Other than that, unless there are specific terms set out in the access order, the visiting parent is free to do with the child what he or she wishes during the access periods. Basically the visiting parent's contact with the child "must be that of a person who visits with her, who spends some time with her, but who cannot change or alter her mode of life or have any general direction of the child's conduct. This is a matter for custody." (*Benoit,* 6 RFL 180 Ont.)

Usually access will take place outside the custodial parent's home, unless again there are specific terms to the contrary. If there is any doubt as to where the access is to take place — inside or outside the custodial parent's home — the judge may be asked to make this specific. Often the custodial parent does not wish a small baby to be taken outside the home. If this is the case, the judge should be asked to articulate this in the custody and access order. Similarly, if for some reason the custodial parent does not wish the visiting parent to take the child beyond certain geographical limits, this should be made specific.

There are no fixed principles about how much access will be awarded to the parent who is not given custody; the disposition of each case will depend on its facts. Generally, though, with younger children less access will be granted, and often it will not include overnight visits. Frequently, if access is not the primary issue in dispute, a judge will simply order "reasonable" access. It is then left to the parties to determine how much access they think is "reasonable." If they cannot agree, then one or the other may bring the matter back to court for specific times to be fixed.

How is access determined?

Usually judges will consider the following:

1. The welfare and happiness of the child are the paramount consideration.
2. Access to the children by the non-custodial parent is almost always granted except in exceptional circumstances, and should not be refused unless danger to the child is apprehended.
3. Although the court will make the final decision, it can and should seek expert advice as to the suitability of each parent and the needs of the child.
4. Many of the factors taken into account in determining the best interest of the child with respect to the issue of custody are also taken into account in determining access. One specific factor is the child's need for stability. (*Stroud,* 18 RFL 237 Ont.)

What exceptional circumstances allow denial of access?

The underlying view is:

> Children are part of the family. They have two parents and have a right to be influenced in their upbringing by each of the two parents. They have a right to the affection of each of the two and while divorce may dissolve the marriage, it does not dissolve the parenthood and the court must be careful not to continue a prohibition against visitation rights except in the most exceptional cases. (*Csicsiri,* 17 RFL 31 Alta.)

Most "exceptional cases" involve some fear of harm to the child, either physical or emotional. In those cases, the judge does not find that it would be in the child's best interests to grant access.

In one case where the mother was mentally and emotionally ill to such an extent that the judge feared she might remove the children from the jurisdiction or possibly injure them "while in the grip of emotional distress," she was denied access. Apparently the court hearing was "frequently interrupted by the screaming, weeping and angry outbursts of the mother. Her testimony was often disjointed and difficult to follow and she laced it with angry demands for explanations as to why various things were taking place or being said." The judge said he reported this in his judgment to point out that she was obviously sick and in need of medical attention. (*Csicsiri,* 13 RFL 263 Alta.) But another mother who had a long history of mental illness, during which time she had hurt the child (the father said it was an attempt at strangulation), was given access. The judge did not think there was reason any longer to fear that she might hurt the child. A psychiatrist testified on her behalf that the mother was now mentally and emotionally normal. In addition, the mother was living with a man who had a fairly substantial criminal record. The judge thought, however, that he was fully rehabilitated and that he was a warm and sensitive person who had a genuine concern for the children. (*Sutherland,* 3 RFL 118 B.C.)

But the mere fact that access may be unsettling to the child, and disturbing to routine, is not enough to bar access; it must be more harmful than that. One judge found emotional disturbance to the child where the evidence showed bitter feuding between the parties over the greater part of the life of the child; the child thought of his stepfather as his real father, and had a reaction close to panic in the presence of his father; the professional reports had concluded that unless an end was put to the constant wrangling, in order to provide an atmosphere of stability for the child, his emotional well-being might be permanently disturbed. (*Stroud,* 18 RFL 237 Ont.) The judge denied access, saying that to preserve the child's emotional welfare, it was better at this juncture to cut off any visiting rights, at least until the child had reached an age where he was able to cope with the situation. Judges will not, however, deny access simply because the child views his custodial parent's new mate as his real father or mother. Nor will access be denied because the custodial parent wants the child to view the new mate as such.

Often during access periods, the visiting parent will criticize the conduct and childraising methods of the custodial parent. If this goes too far, the judge may deny further access. For example, in one case where a mother continually criticized the custodial father, his way of life and his new relationship, and repeatedly admonished her fourteen-year-old daughter for associating with her father's new mate, the judge ended her access rights, saying this was all too disturbing for the daughter. (*Milson,* 11 RFL 250 B.C.)

What conditions will be imposed on visiting rights?
Frequently a judge will grant access even when he has some hesitations about the visiting parent's conduct or situation. In these cases, access will be granted on certain specified terms.

One judge, for example, ordered that the father — the respondent in the divorce — was not to exercise his access rights while in the company of the co-respondent. (*Murray,* 30 RFL 185 N.B.) Another judge, however, refused to impose such terms, saying that since there was a "complete lack of evidence as to the impropriety between the father and his girlfriend and a lack of evidence as to the latter being a person of bad character or one who would have a detrimental influence upon the child," he could see no justification for imposing an absolute prohibition. (*Brown,* 10 RFL 379 Sask.)

Where a father had difficulty with alcohol, the judge ordered him not to consume alcoholic beverages during any time the child was with him, or during the twenty-four hours immediately preceding his access period. In addition, he was not to take the child to any place where other people were consuming alcohol. (*Thomson,* 23 RFL 376 N.B.)

Sometimes, when there is concern that the visiting parent will emotionally or physically harm the child, a term will be imposed stating that the visiting may only take place in the presence of a third person.

If the child has not seen the visiting parent for a considerable period of time, the terms of the access order might allow for graduated visiting — less frequently at first, then more often as time goes by and the child gets used to the visiting parent. Graduated terms are also common in cases of very young children — fewer hours or days at first and then more as the child grows older.

Can a reluctant child be forced to visit with a parent?
Generally courts are of the view that the custodial parent has an obligation to do everything within reason to see that the child will visit with the non-custodial parent. However, the older a reluctant child is, the less likely such visits — even if previously ordered — will be forced by the court, or that the custodial parent will be found in contempt of court.

Access and child support
Normally a parent cannot avoid payment of child support or maintenance simply because of an inability to exercise access rights.

Even where the custodial parent has moved to another province, making it difficult, if not impossible, for the other to exercise his access rights, payments must continue. But in one case where the judge felt the custodial parent was not doing enough within her power to see that her children visited with their father, and in fact seemed to be thwarting such visits, he ordered that payments for the child be suspended as long as the father failed to obtain access to the children. (*Tasson,* 28 RFL 171 Alta.)

Similarly, the custodial parent cannot refuse access simply because the non-custodial parent is in arrears of child support or maintenance.

May the parent with custody leave the jurisdiction?

Access might be ended effectively if the custodial parent moves away. Whether that parent has the right to do so will depend on the wording and interpretation of the custody and access order or agreement. In general, the parent with custody of the children has the right to remove the children without the permission of the other parent, in the absence of some specific agreement or order to the contrary, or in the absence of specific terms with respect to access that clearly indicate that the parties or the judge intended that the children remain in close proximity. If, for example, the order provided that the non-custodial parent was to have the right of access to the children on each and every Saturday, then it must have been intended that the children would reside within such proximity to the non-custodial parent that this access could be implemented. However, where the access is just "reasonable," the custodial parent may move unless there is something else in the agreement or order that indicates the contrary. (*Bruce,* 5 RFL 2nd 198 Ont.)

If you have custody and are considering a move, you should check with a lawyer first. There may be circumstances surrounding your agreement or court order that militate against such a move. You may have to have the agreement or order changed.

Can access be changed?

As with custody, an application may be made to vary access if there has been a material change in circumstances.

Conclusion

Women no longer have a preferred right to custody of the children, nor do they have a preferred obligation. It is not true that just because you are the mother, you must fight for custody or, for the same reason, be automatically awarded custody. Think about this decision carefully before you get involved in a protracted, bitter and costly court battle. Not only will you inevitably come out of such a battle scarred; so will the children.

But if you do make the decision to fight for custody, remember the ultimate test is the best interests of the children. It will be up to you to show the judge that it is in the best interests of the children to be with you.

5.
PROPERTY

One of the most complex issues to be determined on separation or divorce is that of the use and division of property. Who stays in the house? Must the house be sold? If so, how are the proceeds divided? Does the wife get a share of her husband's business, and vice versa? What happens to the stocks, bonds and savings? What happens to the furniture and art? Until quite recently, women have been treated most unfairly by the law and the courts in the settlement of these questions.

The law and practice relating to property rights and property division have changed radically in the last few years. You must remember that laws relating to property are provincial, and therefore vary from province to province. What your rights are and how to enforce them will be determined by the province in which you reside. (Again, Quebec laws are not covered here.)

What is meant by property?

Under the heading of property rights and property division, we include all such items as house, land, money, stocks, bonds, insurance policies, bank accounts, furniture and household items and jewellery. Basically property is money and anything that can be turned into money.

DOES A WOMAN HAVE ANY RIGHT TO HER HUSBAND'S PROPERTY?

In order to understand the implications of recent reform legislation that has changed the law, it helps to have an understanding of the law as it developed in the past. In any event, much of the old law is the foundation on which the reforms have been built, and therefore still applies.

Until the later 1800s, one spouse did get a right to the other's property upon marriage: the right was simply that a woman's property automatically became that of her husband! She was no longer free to deal with her property, her wages or anything else, as her own. She lost all power to sell her property or to use her money as she wished.

Dower and homestead rights

In return, a wife gained a minimal right to her husband's property. It was known as a "dower" right. This simply meant that upon her husband's death, she obtained a one-third interest for the rest of her life in any real estate, or the value thereof, that the husband had owned outright during his life. A wife could voluntarily give up this right to dower on any or all of her husband's property, and in fact often did so in return for something else. For example, upon separation a husband might agree to give his wife monthly support payments in return for her "barring her dower," that is, giving up her dower interest. The wife lost her dower rights if she committed an unforgiven act of adultery during her husband's lifetime. Dower has now been abolished in Ontario and Prince Edward Island.

Alberta, British Columbia, Manitoba and Saskatchewan have a more limited type of dower right that relates solely to the "matrimonial home," the home in which the husband and wife reside. This is called a "homestead" right, and prohibits either spouse from selling the matrimonial home or homestead without the written consent of the other spouse. The homestead laws, except in Saskatchewan, also give the surviving spouse the right to ownership of the home, or the proceeds thereof, for the rest of his or her life.

Married Women's Property Acts and separate property

In the late 1800s, England and then the Canadian provinces, one by one, passed the Married Women's Property Acts. From then on married women had the right to own and deal with property as if they were unmarried. This is often referred to as the "separate property system." Basically it means that what's his is his, and what's hers is hers. With this system, each spouse has a right to acquire and dispose of any property that he or she owns, as he or she wishes. And this does not change upon marriage. That is, marriage no longer gave a husband a right to his wife's income or property. Nor, of course, did it give a wife a right to her husband's.

In the past few years, as we will see below, many provinces have passed reforms dealing with rights of property in marriage. Nonetheless, the separate property system is still the foundation upon which these reforms are based. By and large, the new reforms only apply to rights that spouses acquire on *termination* of the marriage relationship; the separate property system still rules the relationship between the spouses while they are married and living together. In those provinces where no reforms have been passed, the separate property system is still the sole guideline.

WHAT DOES SEPARATE PROPERTY MEAN?

Whose name is the property in?

Usually whoever is named on the title, or has the property in his or her name, has the right to do with that property as he or she wishes. With the exception of the "presumptions" discussed below, it is usually assumed that whoever has title to the property is in fact the owner of that property, and therefore can dispose of it and deal with the proceeds as he or she wishes.

Often, however, it is not clear who is the actual owner of the property. An article might be purchased with funds from both the husband and wife, with little consideration of whether it will belong to one, the other or both, and if to both, in what proportion.

Where there is a dispute about ownership, the deciding factor is who actually paid for the property *and* what the intention as to ownership was at the time of purchase. If, for example, the husband actually pays for the item and intended to have title to it, the property is clearly his. But people rarely keep records or discuss their intentions at the outset, and when a dispute arises they tell conflicting stories about who paid for the property and what the intention was. Before the family property reforms discussed below, there were frequently protracted court battles about ownership of the property. With the reform legislation, these battles are less frequent and not as important. The reforms have bypassed the question of title and ownership, and state that certain divisions will be made notwithstanding ownership. Nonetheless, spouses sometimes wish to determine ownership and the right to use and dispose of property, either before or during the marriage breakdown.

Who owns property the husband has given to the wife and put in her name?

Over the years, the law has developed some "presumptions" or determining rules in deciding who has the right to property. In cases where these presumptions are involved, title, payment or actual intentions are not the only determining factors. One presumption is that of "advancement." If the property is purchased and paid for by the husband, but put in the wife's name, the law presumes that the husband intended to make a gift of the property to his wife. Unless the husband can show convincingly that he intended otherwise, the property belongs to her. This presumption applies only to gifts from husband to wife, not vice versa. As of 1980 the presumption of advancement has been abolished in Ontario, Prince Edward Island, Saskatchewan and Alberta, but is still a guideline in other provinces.

In one case where the husband bought a house and put half of it in the wife's name, but obtained a promissory note from her for half of the house's value, the judge found that the husband clearly did not intend to make an outright gift or advancement to the wife, and he rejected the presumption. The judge held that the husband owned the entire house even though he had put half of it in the wife's name. (*Smith,* 12 RFL 216 B.C.)

In another case, where, as often happens, the husband and wife planned to put the husband's property in the wife's name in order to avoid claims by the husband's creditors, the judge found that the husband had paid for all the property and there was no real intention on his part to make a gift to the wife, so the property belonged to him. (*Sepp,* 22 RFL 76 Ont.)

What rights does the wife gain through financial contribution to property in the husband's name?

Often women make a financial contribution to their husbands' property; for example, the house or a business. In these cases, the law presumes that the husband is thereby holding the whole or a portion of the property in trust for the wife, even if it is not in her name. And where the presumption of advancement has been abolished, the law assumes the same for a husband's contribution to property in the wife's name: she would be holding the whole or a portion in trust for him.

In one case, a wife had provided most of the initial down payment to the family house, which was in the husband's name. The husband made all the mortgage payments. The judge held that the husband was presumed to be holding half of the house in trust for the wife, and she was entitled to half of the proceeds upon its sale. She had made a direct financial contribution to the house and was therefore a part-owner. (*Whiteley,* 16 RFL 309 Ont.)

These ownership disputes can be settled at any time — during the marriage, at separation, at divorce or after. It is simply a question of having a judge determine what one's interest in a particular piece of property is at any given time. The history of the property — its acquisition date, the manner of payment and any discussions between the parties regarding ownership — are presented and the judge will make a determination based on those facts. Accordingly, it is always important to keep accurate records of financial contributions to a property and of one's understanding of the relative ownership interest in it.

What rights does the wife gain through non-financial contribution to a husband's property?

Historically, the most common situations are those where a wife has made indirect financial contributions or contributions of labour to her husband's property or business. These are treated differently than cases of direct financial contribution, such as the ones discussed above. The results have mostly been unfair to wives in this position.

In cases of labour contribution or indirect financial contribution, judges do not presume that the husband is holding a portion of the property in trust for the wife. Given that the property is not in her name, the only question left is whether the courts can find any mutual intention, either express or implied, on the part of both spouses that the property was to be shared.

A typical example of the inequity that befalls a wife who contributes with her labour, but makes no direct financial contribution to her husband's property, is the now infamous *Murdoch* case decided in the Supreme Court in 1973. (13 RFL 185 S.C.C.) When the couple married in Alberta in 1943, the wife owned a few horses, the husband twenty-five to thirty horses and eight cows. They worked together on several ranches until 1947, when the husband and his father-in-law bought a guest ranch, each paying $3,000. There was a dispute about the source of the husband's $3,000, and about whether some of it had come from the joint earnings of the couple. But one thing was clear:

the wife's physical labour. Throughout the marriage, the husband worked in town for about five months of the year; during that time the wife performed the work involved in operating the dude ranch. She accompanied guests on pack trips and fishing and hunting hikes, and did other necessary chores around the ranch. The ranch was sold in 1951 and the husband received $3,500.

Then another property was purchased in the husband's name. Again there was a dispute about the source of the money, but again the extent of the wife's physical labour while the husband was away was clear. That property was sold in 1958 and a larger property, consisting of 480 acres, was purchased in the husband's name. Again the wife did her husband's work during his five months' absence. In summary, the work she did on all the farm properties consisted of haying, raking, swathing, mowing, driving trucks and tractors and teams, quieting horses, taking cattle back and forth to the reserve, dehorning, vaccinating, branding — as Mrs. Murdoch put it, "I worked outside with him, just as a man would, anything that was to be done."

By 1968, the relations between the couple had deteriorated and there was a physical clash that resulted in the wife's hospitalization. They separated; the husband remained in possession of the property and everything in and on it. The wife was left with nothing.

Mrs. Murdoch claimed a share in the property, saying that it was clear from her physical work that there was an implied or unstated agreement that the property was meant to benefit both, that it was to be shared. She said no one would have done all that work who did not believe that the property and farming business was partly hers. The judge, however, said that there was nothing unusual about the work she had done, that she just did what any normal farm wife would do, and that he was not therefore going to infer an intention on the part of the spouses that the property would be owned jointly. If the wife had done something the judge perceived to be more unusual than a normal farm wife's work, he might have inferred such an intention. It is hard to imagine what more she could have done in the circumstances.

In a similar case, where a wife "took care of a garden, canned, made butter, fed chickens, brought lunches and coffee to the field, fetched fuel and machinery parts, took grain samples to the elevator for testing and once in a while drove the farm machinery and picked roots," the judge said there was no express or implied agreement between the parties concerning ownership of the farm property, and thus it remained with the husband, in whose name title had been placed. (*Gerk,* 25 RFL 32 Alta.)

These cases are striking examples of why a woman, before working in her husband's business or on his property, should get an explicit agreement in writing that a share of the business or property, if she so wishes, will belong to her. In these cases one cannot rely on faith, hope, charity or, it seems, reason.

Why Reform?

It became obvious from decisions of this kind by judges that reform was badly needed. Women often assumed unquestioningly that they had a share in the business or property, that their marriage was a partnership and would be recognized as such. Little did they know that indirect financial contribution, to say nothing of direct physical contribution, would not suffice to give them that share.

So several provinces enacted reforms to lessen some of the inequities. As these reforms are very recent, the number of reported cases is relatively small. As with any new law, it is difficult to predict precisely how the enactments will be interpreted, and whether they will benefit women as they are supposed to.

FAMILY ASSETS — ONTARIO, PRINCE EDWARD ISLAND AND BRITISH COLUMBIA

Ontario, Prince Edward Island and British Columbia have enacted legislation saying that when spouses separate, the "family assets" will be divided. This does not mean that the law of "separate property" during marriage has been changed. Husbands and wives are still free during cohabitation to deal with their property as they wish, and the types of property disputes noted above may still occur. But the new legislation states that upon separation there shall be some division of certain property, no matter who owns it. These property reforms only apply to married persons, not to couples living together.

What are "family assets"?

Under the Ontario and Prince Edward Island definitions, any property that is owned by one spouse or both spouses; ordinarily used or enjoyed by both spouses or one or more of their children while the spouses are residing together; and used for shelter or transportation, or for household, education, recreational, social or aesthetic purposes is a family asset. Only items fitting all parts of this definition, or money in a bank account intended for purchasing such items, are subject to division upon separation. In Ontario and Prince Edward Island, then, an insurance policy is not a family asset because it is not used for any of the purposes named. It is true that the intention might be to use it in the future for one of those purposes, but intention is not sufficient to bring it within the definition of a family asset.

The British Columbia act is somewhat broader than the Ontario and Prince Edward Island ones, in that it does include pensions and Registered Retirement Savings Plans (RRSPs). More significantly, it includes businesses if the spouse who does not have title has made a direct or indirect contribution of money or some equivalent. The British Columbia act states that an indirect contribution to a business venture might include "savings through effective management of household or childrearing responsibilities by the spouse who holds no interest in the property." If, for example, a wife liberated money for her husband's business through efficient household management, this is an indirect contribution that makes the business itself a family asset, subject to division.

In one Ontario case where a very wealthy architect named Bregman had a collection of Oriental rugs worth about $200,000, there was a dispute about whether these rugs would fall under the definition of family assets. The architect had more than sixty of these rugs in the matrimonial home, twenty usually on display and forty kept separately, not generally used or displayed in the home. These were preserved for occasional inspection and display to guests and collectors. The judge found that the twenty rugs throughout the home were a family asset, but that the forty segregated rugs were not, since they were maintained separately by the husband and were not ordinarily used or enjoyed by other members of the family. You might question whether a wife's diamond ring kept in a safety deposit box would be a family asset. Is it ordinarily used or enjoyed by both spouses if, in fact, she never wears it? Unlikely.

There was also a dispute in the Bregman case about a Picasso gouache painting, worth $24,000, that had hung in Mr. Bregman's office for a number of years. In 1972, however, he brought it home and placed it in the study, where it was enjoyed by the wife and other members of the family. Then in 1975, about the time it became clear that the marriage was going badly, Mr. Bregman removed the Picasso from the home. The judge found that although the Picasso was not originally a family asset (while it was in Mr. Bregman's office), its status was altered upon its transfer to the matrimonial home and that he could not alter that status again by removing it from the house at the very time the marriage breakdown was imminent.

A further twist regarding the Picasso was that it was actually owned by Mr. Bregman's company, a company that was wholly owned by him. But this was not an obstacle to its being a family asset, since the legislation provides that an item can be a family asset even when owned by a corporation. Instead of dividing such an item itself, the court will divide the number of shares in the corporation that represent the value of the family asset. (*Bregman,* 7 RFL 2nd 201 Ont.)

In another case, a wife owned and displayed an immense doll collection, worth about $25,000, that the court found not to be a family asset. The wife had used the doll collection as a financial venture and not for any of the purposes necessary to make the collection a family asset. (*Boydell,* 2 RFL 2nd 121 Ont.)

It must be remembered that in Ontario and Prince Edward Island, a family asset must be used by *both* spouses or by one or more of the children. It is not enough that it is used by just one spouse. Thus, a boat that only the husband sails, the wife and children never going on it, is not a family asset.

Also, the item must be used ordinarily by the spouses. It is not enough that it is intended to be used in the future. In one case where the husband had purchased a condominium in Florida and the wife had been there on a few occasions to help decorate it, with the intention that it would be leased at first and later used as a recreational property, the judge found that the condominium was not a family asset. It was not ordinarily used for recreational purposes even though there was an intention to do so. (*Taylor,* 6 RFL 2nd 341 Ont.)

A wife should never assume that she will get a share of whatever seems in the ordinary sense to be a family asset. Before it becomes a family asset in law, it must be ordinarily used as such by both spouses or by the children, for the specifically named purposes. But it does not matter whether the asset was acquired before or during marriage.

When are the family assets divided?

All three provinces made the reforms retroactive so they apply to all marriages, even those that took place before the reforms were enacted. (There are ways of contracting out of the reforms, however, that are discussed in chapters 2 and 7, on marriage contracts and separation agreements.) It is essential to keep in mind that the concept of separate property is still intact. Family assets do not mean community property, joint ownership or anything like that. They simply provide that when certain events happen, either spouse may receive a division of the family assets, regardless of ownership. But until those events the law of separate property still applies.

Generally, a division of family assets can be applied for once the parties are separated with no reasonable prospect of reconciliation. The fact that one spouse deserted the other has no bearing on the division. The parties can agree on their own how to divide the family assets, but if there is a dispute, an application can be made to a court, on its own or at the time of the divorce hearing. In Ontario and Prince Edward Island, the application must be made while the parties are still married; in British Columbia, it is allowed within two years of a divorce.

Only the properties defined as family assets that exist at the time of separation are subject to division. Because something may have been a family asset ten years ago — for example, a cottage that has since been sold — that does not mean that the proceeds from its sale will now be divided. Furthermore, only family *assets* are divided, or more precisely the net value of the assets. Family *debts* are not divided and continue to belong to whomever incurred them.

Finally, if one of the spouses dies, there will be no division of family assets. At death, the deceased's property goes to whomever he or she wanted. The surviving spouse does not have a share under the reform legislation in what might have been the family assets.

Can the husband sell a potential family asset at the time of separation?

You need not worry that your husband will sell the family home, even if it's in his name alone. The legislation requires that both spouses give their consent to such a sale. It is very unlikely, therefore, that a third party would buy a home without the written consent of both parties, and even if this occurred the sale could be set aside.

However, there is nothing preventing either spouse from selling other property if he or she wishes, although the legislation provides that you may get a court order stopping such a sale until the division of family assets has been resolved. This should always be done if you get any indication of an impending sale. Although the judge can take into account the proceeds your husband would receive on the sale of a family asset, by the time you get to court, he may have spent that money. It is always better to keep the property intact.

How does the wife know what assets the husband has?
Most enactments require that upon application for a division of the family assets you must file under oath a complete statement of your own property and its net worth. In return, your spouse must file a similar statement. Since these statements are made under oath, one would be committing perjury by not revealing *all* property in which one has an interest. Where no such statement is required, the extent of a husband's assets might not be determined until pre-trial proceedings.

In what proportion are the family assets divided?
Basically the family assets are to be divided equally. However, all three provinces with this kind of legislation allow the judge to make an unequal division of family assets where an equal division would, in his judgment, be inequitable. In Ontario and Prince Edward Island, the judge can consider, for example, the length of cohabitation, the date when the property was acquired, the extent to which the property was acquired by one spouse, by inheritance or by gift, and "any other circumstance relating to the acquisition, disposition, preservation, maintenance, improvement or use of the property, rendering it inequitable for the division of family assets to be in equal shares." Say a widow remarries and her new husband moves into the home that she has owned for twenty years, and after a few months their marriage falls apart. It is quite likely that the court will not make an equal division of the home, but rather, considering the period of cohabitation and the date of acquisition, give the second husband a share much smaller than fifty percent.

A judge in British Columbia has similar discretion to make an unequal division and may consider "the needs of each spouse to become or remain economically independent and self-sufficient." A judge might be persuaded that a wife should get a larger share than fifty percent of the family assets if, for example, her income-earning ability is much smaller than her husband's. The judge might consider that she will need more of the assets to embark on and continue a retraining program in order to become economically independent and self-sufficient.

How are the family assets actually shared?

A judge need not order that the assets be sold and the proceeds divided equally. Often this would be cumbersome and inappropriate. Instead he can order that a certain property be transferred to one spouse, another property to the other. Or he can order that one spouse pay to the other a sum of money for the purpose of adjusting the division. Thus if a house has an equity of $40,000 and the wife wishes to remain in it, the judge might order that she pay the husband $20,000 in settlement of his share of that family asset. Or where there is a house with an equity of $40,000 and remaining family assets worth $40,000, the judge might order that the house be transferred to one spouse and the remaining family assets to the other.

If the property is outside the province, the judge can take the value of that property into account in determining the division. He cannot, however, order that property sold, as judges exercising jurisdiction under provincial laws have no power over property outside their particular province.

What happens to non-family assets?

Non-family assets are anything other than family assets. The British Columbia act makes no provision whatsoever for sharing in non-family assets; however, the British Columbia definition of family assets is much broader than the one in the Ontario and Prince Edward Island acts.

Ontario and Prince Edward Island have provisions whereby a judge may dip into the non-family assets in certain circumstances. If a spouse has unreasonably impoverished the family assets, the judge might look to that spouse's non-family assets and order a division of or contribution from them. In addition, if the judge considers that a division of the family assets alone is inequitable given certain circumstances, he might dip into the family assets. These circumstances include, for example, the date of acquisition of the property and the length of cohabitation. If the spouses have lived together for thirty years and acquired non-family assets worth $100,000, whereas the husband has acquired family assets worth $400,000, the judge might consider a division of the family assets alone inequitable. Such a division would leave the wife only $50,000, whereas the husband would retain $450,000. In that case, the judge might give the wife some of the husband's non-family assets.

The judge might also consider the effect of one party's assuming responsibility for child care and household management on the ability of the other spouse to acquire, manage, maintain, operate or improve property that is not a family asset. In the *Bregman* case discussed earlier, the wife was given a share of her husband's non-family assets when the judge considered that criterion. The judge found as follows:

> After Mrs. Bregman ceased to work in 1951, the couple assumed the traditional roles of husband and wife. Mr. Bregman established and extended his practice and acquired ultimately substantial investments; he was the bread-winner. Mrs. Bregman assumed the role of managing the household and the care and upbringing of the children; in the latter activity Mr. Bregman made an appropriate contribution as a good husband and father. This left him free to pursue his commercial career unencumbered by time- and-energy consuming duties. He provided the financing of the household; she managed it. He was a generous husband. He provided a joint bank account, upon her use of which he seems to have placed little limitation. She paid the bills from it. He provided a series of full-time housekeepers and a part-time charwoman. This does not, however, reduce Mrs. Bregman's responsibility for household management and child care. The domestics were simply her assistants, whom she supervised in carrying out her role in the marriage partnership. Mr. Bregman very fairly acknowledged that he had no criticism of her as a wife and mother, and that without her contribution he could not have achieved the success that he has, especially in the early years when he was becoming established. . . . She was . . . the marriage partner who took the main burden of responsibility for household management and child care. I am in no doubt that this left her husband physically, intellectually and mentally free to concentrate as much as he required on earning money and acquiring and managing the non-family assets.

In this case, the accumulation of non-family assets by the husband was significantly in excess of family assets, and the judge therefore found that some further distribution of non-family assets was necessary to recognize adequately the wife's contribution to their acquisition by the performance of her domestic role. Therefore after dividing the family assets of $655,000 in equal shares, giving Mrs. Bregman more than $327,000, the judge further awarded her non-family assets to the extent of $300,000, ordering Mr. Bregman to pay her that sum. (Mr. Bregman's net worth was admitted to be $2.8 million.) (*Bregman,* 7 RFL 2nd 201 Ont.)

There is no set formula for the share a spouse might get in non-family assets. In one case where the wife assumed the major burden of raising the children and running the house, and also economized so that funds that might otherwise have contributed to a higher standard of living for the family were used to build the husband's landscaping business, the judge, in addition to dividing the family assets equally, felt that a fair disposition would be to give the wife twenty percent of the husband's landscaping business and property. He valued the business and property and then ordered the husband to pay the wife twenty percent of that value. (*Kastrau,* 7 RFL 2nd 318 Ont.)

Other ways to get non-family assets

Even if the judge will not dip into the non-family assets in the way described in the *Bregman* and *Kastrau* cases above, a spouse might still make a claim by another avenue to the non-family assets. In Ontario and Prince Edward Island, the legislation has provided what is known as a "Murdoch clause." This allows a spouse or former spouse to make a claim for a share of the non-family assets where he or she has "contributed work, money or monies worth in respect of the acquisition, management, maintenance, operation or improvement of the property in which the other has or had an interest." The judge may direct payment of an amount in compensation for the contribution or award a share in the property itself. The legislation goes on to say that the judge shall assess the contribution without regard to the relationship of husband and wife, or to the fact that the acts constituting the contribution are those of a reasonable spouse of that sex in the circumstances. You will remember that the judge in the *Murdoch* case said there was nothing special about the work Mrs. Murdoch had done, since it was simply what any farm wife would have done in the circumstances; the legislation in Ontario and Prince Edward Island specifically tells judges to disregard that line of reasoning in the future. Thus if Mrs. Murdoch had lived in Ontario and her claim had been made after the enactment of the new legislation, she probably would have received a share of her husband's farming business or some other settlement. She had clearly contributed "work" in respect of the management, maintenance and operation of the business, and the fact that she had done "what any farm wife would do" would have been irrelevant.

Often wives work in their husbands' stores or offices, and this provision provides for them to have a share in those businesses, or payment in compensation. In the *Bregman* case, the wife made a claim under this section of the legislation as well as the one previously discussed. However, the judge found that some clerical work by the wife in the early years of the husband's business was not significant enough to order a share via this avenue. In the *Boydell* case above, the husband was awarded $1,500 as a share in the wife's doll collection, as he had built the doll cabinets and regularly drove his wife around to buy or sell the dolls. Thus he had contributed "work" and was entitled to some compensation from the business.

Similarly, where a wife had consented to a mortgage on the family home, the money from the mortgage being used for the husband's business, she was given compensation since she had, through the mortgage, contributed "monies worth" — part of her interest in the matrimonial home — to his business.

OTHER REFORM PROVINCES — ALBERTA, SASKATCHEWAN AND MANITOBA

Alberta and Manitoba have passed matrimonial property reforms, but these vary from the family-asset systems discussed so far. Saskatchewan has passed reform legislation, but at this writing it has not become effective because it has not been proclaimed. (The remaining provinces and territories have not yet enacted changes as of 1980, so that the law discussed in the beginning pages of this chapter is all that applies. However, reforms were being considered in other provinces and may even be enacted by the time you read this book.) Once again, the reforms in these provinces maintain the separate property system *during* marriage but provide for division of property when the marriage breaks down. They only apply to married persons.

Alberta

In Alberta *all* property belonging to either or both spouses is subject to division, except for (a) property acquired before the marriage, (b) property acquired by gift or inheritance, (c) insurance proceeds or (d) damages received as a result of what is termed a tort proceeding in court (for example, damages arising out of a motor vehicle accident). Either spouse may make an application for division of property upon separation or divorce, or even prior to that time if the other spouse has transferred or intends to transfer or make a gift of property with the intention of defeating the applicant's claim. Any application must, however, be made within two years of divorce.

Basically a judge in Alberta will order an equal division of all property unless it would not be "just and equitable" to do so. In determining whether an unequal division should be made, the judge can look at thirteen factors including "any fact or circumstance that is relevant." Among other things, he can look at:

1. the contribution made by each spouse to the marriage and to the welfare of the family, including any contribution made as a homemaker or parent;

2. the income-earning capacity, liabilities, obligations, property and other financial resources
(a) that each spouse had at the time of the marriage, and
(b) that each spouse has at the time of the trial;

3. the contribution, whether financial or in some other form, made directly or indirectly [to] the property.

Such discretion in the hands of the judge means of course that one can never be sure of receiving half of the property or value thereof, and that court proceedings may be long and complicated. These criteria create the possibility that the whole history of the marriage will be examined, not just financial details.

Alberta judges have the same discretion as the judges in the provinces discussed previously in the types of decisions they can make — property can be transferred, payments can be ordered, or any other order can be made to adjust a division.

Saskatchewan

The Saskatchewan reform also covers any property acquired after marriage, with certain exceptions such as insurance proceeds. Once again, the property is to be divided equally upon marriage breakdown or death, unless the judge thinks it would be "unfair or inequitable" to do so. Unlike the situation in the other provinces, the judges can make the division at *any* time, even before marriage breakdown.

Manitoba

Manitoba's legislation divides assets into family assets, using a definition similar to Ontario's, and commercial assets — all other assets. However, the definitions are limited to those assets acquired during the marriage. In addition, some assets are excluded, such as gifts to one spouse and insurance proceeds. Upon marriage breakdown or the death of a spouse (if the spouses were already separated), the division of all relevant property is to be equal, with certain exceptions. In the case of family assets, the judge can order an unequal division, but only where division in equal shares would be "grossly unfair or unconscionable having regard to any extraordinary financial or other circumstances of the spouses or the extraordinary nature or value of any of the assets."

The judge may also make an unequal division of commercial assets, and here the criteria are broader and more likely to lead to such division. The judge may consider, among other things, the amount of debts and liabilities of each spouse and the circumstances in which they were incurred; the length of cohabitation during marriage; and the extent to which the financial means and earning capacity of each spouse has been affected by the responsibilities and other circumstances of the marriage. The Manitoba property reforms do not apply to spouses living separate and apart on or before 6 May 1977.

WHAT HAPPENS TO THE FAMILY OR MATRIMONIAL HOME?

The matrimonial home is considered to be the home, apartment or other dwelling occupied by the spouses as their family residence. Wives often have specific concerns about their right to the matrimonial home: will they get any share of the proceeds when the home is sold; do they have the right to remain in the home if the parties separate; do they have the right to have the husband ordered out of the home in intolerable situations?

Will the wife get a share of the sale proceeds?
Traditionally, if the home was not in the wife's name, or at least in her name jointly with her husband's, she had no right to any part of the proceeds when the home was sold. This often came as a shock to a woman who had lived and worked in the home and maintained it over the years. However, the only way she could expect any share in the proceeds was if she could show the judge that a portion of the home was being held in trust for her because of her financial contribution. In addition, if the wife lived in one of the western provinces that had "homestead" legislation, she had some leverage for demanding a share of the proceeds, in that her consent was needed for any sale of the house.

Now with the various reform laws it is not as important that a wife show a title or ownership interest in the home. She will probably get a share of the proceeds simply by the division of family or other assets. Ontario and Prince Edward Island, for example, make it very clear that the matrimonial home is a "family asset," and several judges have said that only in the most unusual cases should the division be other than fifty/fifty.

Can the wife have her husband ordered out of the matrimonial home?
A judge has always been able to stop the husband from entering the matrimonial home or order him out of it. In other words, he would give the wife the right to "exclusive possession." This power was based not on any specific legislation, but simply on a judge's inherent right to protect the remaining members of the family. Judges' views of what would warrant such a restraining order or injunction varied from time to time and from province to province, but generally, if a judge was of the view that the wife's or children's life or well-being was in danger, he would order the husband to remain away. Some judges did not even look to violent behaviour on the part of the husband, but simply to an extremely intolerable situation. In one case where there was constant arguing between the husband and wife, the husband continually telling the children that the wife was crazy and in general making the home an intolerable place to live, the judge ordered the husband excluded. He based this order on the welfare of the children.

> If it were not for the children, I would not consider granting an injunction. . . . This is a drastic remedy and is not available to the one spouse

> merely because the presence of the other spouse causes unpleasantness, inconvenience and tension. The fact is, however, that for the children of the marriage, life has become intolerable and . . . it is not right or proper that they should be expected to live under extreme tension, merely because there is no likelihood of violence. (*Visscher,* 6 RFL 392 B.C.)

This remedy of a restraining order or injunction is still available in those provinces where no specific legislation has been passed dealing with the spouses' rights to possession of the matrimonial home.

What are the wife's rights to possession of the home?

Traditionally, a "separated" wife's right to stay in the home was protected even before the new legislation. A "deserted" spouse had a right to remain in possession of the home until the time of divorce. Thus if a husband deserted his wife without any cause, the wife could remain in the home until a court ordered otherwise.

In their reform legislation, Ontario and Prince Edward Island have clearly articulated that spouses have equal rights to possession of the matrimonial home, and that the home cannot be sold or in any way dealt with without the consent of both spouses. Thus even if the home is in the husband's name alone, he cannot sell it without the consent of the wife. Nor can he put a mortgage on the house or in any other way encumber it without the wife's consent.

The legislation also allows a judge to make an order of exclusive possession, ordering that one spouse must leave the home or stay out of it. This order can only be made if "other provision for shelter is not adequate in the circumstances," or if it is in the best interests of a child to do so. In applications for exclusive possession, it is always useful to have a medical report stating the effect of the husband's behaviour on the wife and/or children.

Often when the situation in the household is extremely tense, a wife will bring an application for exclusive possession at the same time as she brings a divorce proceeding and an application for division of assets. Just as in divorce proceedings concerning interim support and custody, she can also get a short-term order for exclusive possession until the final trial.

In situations of extreme emergency, the wife might bring an application for exclusive possession without even serving the papers on her husband. In one case where in the previous three weeks the husband had drunkenly assaulted his wife twice and threatened her with a knife, the judge granted her what is called an "*ex parte* exclusive possession order." The judge said, "It does not seem equitable for her to live in a state of perpetual fear in the same house with the respondent [husband], if she were required to serve him with notice of proceedings which are certain to antagonize him, thereby jeopardizing her safety further." (*Busse,* 2 RFL 2nd 273 Ont.)

In Alberta, the judge has broad discretionary powers to order one spouse out of the house and to give exclusive possession to the other. In doing so, he must consider the availability of other accommodation with the means of each spouse, the needs of any children residing in the matrimonial home, and the financial position of each of the spouses. Other provinces, such as British Columbia and Manitoba, also give a judge the right to make an order for exclusive possession, although the criteria are not as explicit.

Conclusion

More than in any other area of family law, in property the law is both complex and precise. The old law dovetails with the reforms, the reforms are technical and lengthy, and the reforms vary from province to province. But if you understand the basic concepts, such as separate property and family assets, you will be much better equipped to arrange and deal with your situation, both during marriage and after. At the very least, keep records of all direct and indirect financial contributions you make to any of your husband's property.

Never rely on informal arrangements or unspoken assumptions. Do not assume, no matter what your husband or anyone else tells you, that half of anything or everything is yours. If you do not have the right to half of something in law — for example, your husband's Canada Savings Bonds — and you think you should, get it in writing. If you do not, you may be sorry later on and you may spend a lot of time and money finding that out.

6.
SUPPORT AND MAINTENANCE

There are two forms of financial assistance for which a wife can ask her husband. The first, called support, can be requested before the marriage is dissolved, while the parties are still legally married but separated; the second, maintenance, is requested at the time of a divorce.

Whether a wife will want financial support, at least for herself, will depend on many factors: her means at the time of separation; the standard of living she has become accustomed to during the marriage; her financial needs; her age and health; the length of the marriage; her future prospects for financial independence; her contribution through her role in the marriage to her husband's financial position; and her husband's financial needs and means. Depending on the relationship between the parties and their individual circumstances, these factors will take on more or less weight. Because of the economic position of women in society — their relatively higher rate of unemployment and lower wages, as well as the role of homemaker and childraiser that women have traditionally had in marriage — they are frequently not in a position to be economically independent from their husbands upon marriage breakdown. Economic independence does not necessarily follow legal independence. This is particularly true if there are children, and it is very rare that women can forgo child support even if they decide or are forced to forgo support for themselves.

Can a wife get support without getting a divorce?

If there are no grounds for divorce or neither party wishes to sue for divorce, there are still ways in which you may get financial support. (Support for children will be dealt with separately, later in this chapter.) Each province has laws that allow a wife to apply for support upon separation of the parties but before divorce. These break down into two types: those provinces in which some matrimonial misconduct, some "fault" on your husband's part, is required before you may apply for support; and those provinces in which mere separation is sufficient for such an application.

Matrimonial misconduct provinces — Alberta, Saskatchewan, New Brunswick, Nova Scotia, Newfoundland and the Yukon and Northwest Territories

The legislation in these provinces is known as "deserted wives" legislation. Applications in these provinces can only be made while the parties are still married and apply only to married persons, not to those living common-law. The only exception is in Newfoundland, where a "wife" is defined to include a woman who has lived continuously with a man who is not her husband, as husband and wife, for not less than one year preceding the application for support, and who has given birth to a child of the union. In these provinces, a deserted wife may immediately bring an application for support after a certain event happens, namely "desertion."

What is desertion?

Failure to provide with food or necessaries. Under some laws, for example in Saskatchewan, desertion might be deemed to exist even if the husband and wife are still living together, but the husband is failing, without sufficient cause, to provide the wife with food or other necessaries. Or if a wife has left her husband because of such refusal or neglect, she is deemed deserted. If, however, the husband has little or no money, then he would have "sufficient cause" for not providing his wife with food or other necessaries and she would not be deserted.

Simple desertion. If a husband has simply left his wife without any cause, then she is deserted. If his wife needs money immediately, an application to the courts for support may be the only vehicle through which she could obtain it. If her husband has done nothing other than desert her, she has to wait three years for a divorce, but through these provincial laws she can bring an application for support immediately. If he has left her for cause, for example her adultery, she is not considered to be deserted, and what happens in this situation is discussed below.

Cruelty. A wife is also deemed to be deserted if she is living apart from her husband because of his cruelty. Cruelty is defined in some of the provincial acts. Generally it is conduct much more serious than the cruelty discussed in chapter 3 on divorce. In Saskatchewan, it means

> conduct creating a danger to life, limb or health or any course of conduct that in the opinion of the court is grossly insulting and intolerable, or is of such a character without proof of actual personal violence, that the wife or children seeking maintenance could not reasonably be expected to be willing to live with the husband or parent after he has been guilty of same.

Husband's adultery. A wife is also deemed to be deserted if she is living apart from her husband because of his uncondoned acts of adultery. The proof of this is the same as proof of adultery in divorce proceedings.

Can a husband apply for support in these provinces?

The "deserted wives" acts generally apply only to wives. Husbands cannot apply for support under these acts, except in Alberta and Newfoundland.

Alimony

You will often hear the term "alimony." It is basically the support a deserted wife can obtain before divorce, and the grounds are virtually identical to those set out in "deserted wives" legislation. The only difference is that an application for alimony is brought in a superior or supreme court of the province, rather than in a family or provincial court.

Alimony actions still exist in the above-named provinces, as well as in British Columbia and Manitoba. They have been abolished in Ontario and Prince Edward Island.

Wife's adultery

A wife who has committed an uncondoned act of adultery is barred from getting support under the "deserted wives" legislation and in alimony actions. The bar concerning adultery applies even after a support order is made. If a husband finds out that his wife subsequently commits adultery, he can bring the case back to court and have the payments terminated.

The only exception is in New Brunswick. There the judge must be satisfied that her adultery is actually the cause of the husband's desertion or refusal to maintain her. If that was not the case, then a wife who is living apart from her husband, but who has in fact committed adultery, may still get support.

NO-FAULT PROVINCES — ONTARIO, PRINCE EDWARD ISLAND, BRITISH COLUMBIA AND MANITOBA

It became apparent with the "deserted wives" legislation and alimony actions that considerable and unnecessary fault-finding was required for a wife to get support. The whole history of the marriage had to be examined, and witnesses called as to cruelty, adultery or desertion. Often the economic factors were given too little weight or simply overlooked. Accordingly, a number of provinces have recently passed legislation that does not require any "fault" or "desertion" to be shown before the issue of support can be determined. Upon separation, a wife can simply apply for support, and although a number of factors are considered, conduct, if considered at all, is relatively unimportant.

When can the wife bring a claim for support?

In Ontario, Prince Edward Island and British Columbia, the legislation now states clearly that every spouse has an obligation to provide support for himself or herself *and* for the other spouse, in accordance with need, to the extent that he or she is capable of doing so. The Manitoba legislation, while not as clear, has a similar provision.

How much will the wife get?

In the "deserted wives" and alimony actions, the court, once it has determined there are grounds for an order, will look at the needs and means of the parties and make an order accordingly. In the "no-fault" provinces, several factors are set out for the courts to consider. In Ontario and Prince Edward Island, the judge may consider sixteen factors. Some of the most significant ones are:

1. the assets and means of the dependant (the person applying for support);
2. the capacity of the dependant to provide for his or her own support;
3. the capacity of the respondent (the person who is being asked to provide support) to provide support;

4. the age, physical and mental health of the dependant and the respondent;
5. the length of time the dependant and respondent cohabited;
6. the needs of the dependant. To determine this, the court may have regard to the accustomed standard of living while the parties resided together;
7. the measures available for the dependant to become financially independent, and the length of time and cost required to enable the dependant to take such measures;
8. the desirability of having the dependant or respondent remain at home to care for a child;
9. a contribution by the dependant to the realization of the career potential of the respondent;
10. the effect on the dependant's earning capacity of the responsibilities assumed during cohabitation;
11. any housekeeping, child care or other domestic service performed by the spouse for the family, to be considered as if the spouse were devoting that time to remunerative employment instead, and were contributing the earnings therefrom to the support of the family.

British Columbia and Manitoba have similar provisions, although not as many in number.

These criteria are very clearly economic. They address the necessary issues, rather than who broke up the marriage and why. They also take into account the detrimental economic position women have traditionally assumed in marriage. It is quite common for a woman to assist her husband's education and career development to the neglect of her own financial independence. Factor 9 recognizes this "division of labour," and directs the judge to consider it when determining the amount of support. Similarly, where a wife has fulfilled the role of homemaker to the detriment of her own financial independence, the judge will look at items 10 and 11. Often items 9, 10 and 11 are one and the same, in that by staying home and taking care of the house, the wife contributes to the husband's career. In one typical case where the wife's primary function throughout the marriage had been as homemaker and supportive wife, the judge awarded her support based on items 10 and 11. He said:

> I should think . . .that the [wife's]faithful performance of her duties as

> a wife might be recognized financially in the form of maintenance. . . . Mrs. Taylor has played second fiddle to Mr. Taylor in terms of advancement and self-improvement over the whole course of the marriage. It was in the role of supportive spouse and homemaker that she gave him an opportunity to advance from job to job, to improve his business and develop his business contacts. It is noteworthy that the monies which she received in the form of salary . . . [as a bookkeeper, when she did outside work] were spent solely on the family rather than on investment. She has lost the better part of her most productive years in raising her family and helping her husband. Now in her middle years . . . she finds herself with her children grown, her husband gone, and her prospects for advancement somewhat dim. One can understand her bitterness. In the course of the marriage, her husband, with her help, dramatically increased his earning potential and his standard of living. She, however, stood still in that regard. (*Taylor,* 6 RFL 2nd 341 Ont.)

The judge then went on to say that having regard to the length of cohabitation (item 5), and the ability of the wife to earn a reasonable income (item 2),

> it would appear appropriate to compensate [the wife] for her lost opportunities of advancement and her contribution to the career potential of her husband by assessing maintenance in her favour in a way which would equalize the spouses' income potentials.

In taking into account item 2, the capacity of the wife to provide her own support, the judge noted that she had once worked as a bookkeeper. She had quit that job and at the time of the trial was not working. Nonetheless, based on her previous salary of $150 weekly, he assumed she could earn $7,800 yearly. He also took into account the impending sale of the matrimonial home, in which each party would net about $70,000 (item 1). If invested, this would produce a yearly income of approximately $6,300 for each. Then, based on the husband's income of $29,000, the judge awarded the wife the sum of $900 monthly.

The wife had indicated at the trial that she wanted to embark on a fresh career in interior design, and for that she would need re-education and more support from her husband. The judge, however, dismissed this factor (item 7). No information had been given about her prospects if she were to become an interior designer, nor as to her aptitude in this area. She would have been much better advised to come to court with very concrete plans and information about her proposed re-education. She should have brought application forms, course interviews, information on starting and future salary and cost and length of such re-education.

How much does the wife need?

Generally in these applications, both parties fill out expense sheets, indicating exactly how much money they will need monthly to carry on. These are used as the basis for the ultimate award. The other side, of course, tries to minimize the proposed expenses by cross-examining on various items. For instance, if a wife says she will need $300 a month for clothing, you can be sure that her husband's lawyer will cross-examine her on this. He will ask how much she has spent on clothing in the past, what sort of clothing she has bought recently, and whether those purchases weren't frivolous. You are well advised to come prepared with receipts from past purchases, so that you can justify whatever expenses you may be claiming, and show your past standard of living. If your expenses, for example housing, are going to change, you should have exact information about the new costs. Be able to substantiate as much as possible what you are claiming.

All the provinces with no-fault support legislation require that both parties file sworn statements fully disclosing all their income, assets and debts.

How is conduct a factor in these provinces?

The no-fault provinces only allow the court to consider conduct as a factor in determining the *amount* of support. Conduct is not a factor in determining whether one should get support but simply how much. In addition, any conduct considered relevant must be "so unconscionable as to constitute an obvious and gross repudiation of the relationship." This must be very severe matrimonial misconduct, generally more severe than in the cruelty cases in chapter 3 on divorce. So far, there have been very few cases where the judges have considered the conduct so "unconscionable" as to affect the award of support.

What is the position of a working wife?

Judges are increasingly reluctant to believe that wives cannot earn an income. If they have any indication that a wife has some ability, either through education or past working experience, to hold a job, they will take this into account in assessing support. Judges are not always cognizant of the difficulty encountered by women who have been off the job market for many years; if you are in this position, evidence should be produced, either through rejected application forms or from an economist or other social scientist, to prove the difficulties. You must show the judge that economic opportunities and economic equality have not necessarily followed legal equality.

Support orders can be made for a specific number of years. If you are planning a retraining program, you might ask for support at least until it is finished, perhaps with a lesser amount thereafter. Since you can never be sure of obtaining an adequately paying job, even when the retraining is completed, some provision should be made for that contingency.

What kinds of orders can be made?
Generally provincial orders are "periodic." That is, they are expressed as weekly or monthly payments. The spouse receiving these periodic payments must pay income tax on them, so you must remember that in fact you will have less available than the amount awarded. Conversely, the party paying support can deduct those payments from taxable income. This usually operates as a considerable tax advantage, in that it puts him or her in a lower tax bracket. Payments are only taxable or deductible, however, if made pursuant to a court order or written separation agreement. If simply paid voluntarily, and not incorporated into a written separation agreement, they are not subject to the same taxation or deduction.

The judge can also order that a lump-sum payment be made, either on its own or in conjunction with periodic payments. Lump-sum payments are not taxable or deductible. The criteria of when lump-sum payments are ordered will be discussed further on. In addition, the judge can order that certain property be transferred to satisfy support orders; that an insurance policy designate a dependant as beneficiary; and that the order be a debt on a respondent's estate for a certain period of time.

The judge can make the order retroactive to any date before the order, for example from the date the parties actually separated, and can make the order effective for a specific period of time, for example five years. On the other hand, the judge might not name a termination date at all; if no other order is made at the time of the divorce, the support order will continue.

Divorce and maintenance

As discussed earlier, the divorce court judge can order at the time of granting a divorce that either spouse pay financial support to the other, for the spouse or for the children. Support ordered after a divorce is called maintenance.

If the amount of maintenance were determinable by a mathematical formula, there would not be the myriad of fights and decisions on whether maintenance should be paid and if so, how much. It used to be thought that on divorce a wife would get one-third of her husband's income. But as one judge said, the one-third rule "is no longer, if it ever was, a useful guide, even as a rough rule of thumb. I think that it does not ordinarily reflect the reality of needs and incomes in our society." (*MacIsaac,* 17 RFL 328 N.S.)

Is conduct throughout the marriage considered?

The Divorce Act says that a judge may, if he thinks it fit and just to do so *having regard to the conduct of the parties* and the condition, means and other circumstances of each of them, make an order requiring payment of maintenance by either the husband or the wife. The judge will look at the conduct of the parties throughout the marriage, not just its final years. As well as looking at the contributions that each party made to the marriage — that is, conduct in its broader sense — he will also look at the misconduct of either party.

In one case, where a judge was of the view that it was solely the wife's misconduct (in that case, adultery) that caused the marriage breakdown, he reduced by forty percent the award he said he would have given to a "blameless" wife. (*Guy,* 9 RFL 238 N.S.) But such an arithmetical deduction is very rare. Often conduct is mentioned in a judge's decision, but the exact weight it is given is indeterminable.

It is especially difficult to assess what weight, if any, will be placed on the misconduct of a husband. In one case where a man had treated his wife with extreme cruelty, the wife asked for a higher maintenance payment than she might have under other circumstances. The judge refused, saying: "I know of cases in which wives have, because of misconduct, been deprived in a sterner age of maintenance, but I know of no case in which a guilty party to a divorce suit has been ordered to pay higher maintenance by way of punishment for his misconduct." (*Chequer,* 9 RFL 208 B.C.)

Another judge said, "When engaged in assessing maintenance, one does not include as a contributing factor any element of punitive damage for marital misconduct, no matter how great. To do so would in effect be imposing punishment in assessing the fine to be paid to the wife; a very different thing from fixing maintenance." (*Osbourne,* 14 RFL 61 B.C.)

Adultery

The fact that a wife has committed adultery is not a bar to her receiving maintenance. This is totally different from a wife's claim to maintenance for alimony, in those provinces that still have such a claim, or for a "deserted" wife's claim in the "fault" provinces. However, the adultery is "conduct" that the judge will consider and take into account in determining maintenance.

In one case, where a wife had not only committed adultery but was living with another man at the time of the divorce, the judge would not grant her periodic maintenance. He did, however, order her husband to make a lump-sum payment. The judge said that he could bring himself to award a lump-sum payment, since that in a sense was a recognition of her contribution to the marriage, but "to impose upon a man an obligation to provide periodic maintenance to his former wife who is living with another man is to make a mockery of basic social principles. While I acknowledge the jurisdiction of the court to make such an imposition, I will not exercise that jurisdiction except in remarkable circumstances." This same judge was of the view that "to foster, endorse or encourage common-law relationships is to diminish the presence of the family unit in our society and anything which diminishes that presence diminishes our society." (*Chaffey,* 3 RFL 2nd 69 Nfld.)

Condition, means and other circumstances

As well as conduct, the judge must consider "condition, means and other circumstances." Judges include under this heading the assets and means of the spouses, their needs, and their standards of living throughout the marriage. The guidelines below, while based on a particular case where the judge found the husband had broken up the marriage, are considered in a variety of other divorce situations as well. You will see that the standard of living and the wife's income are given considerable weight:

1. In cohabitation, a wife and the children share with the husband the standard of living appropriate to his income, or, if the wife is also working, their joint incomes.
2. Where cohabitation has been disrupted by a matrimonial offence on the part of the husband (for example, adultery), the wife's and children's maintenance should be so assessed that their standard of living does not suffer more than is inherent in the circumstances of separation, though the standards may be lower than theretofore (since the income or incomes may now have to support two households in place of the former one where household expenses were shared). Therefore, although the standard of living of all parties may have to be lower than before there was a breach of cohabitation, in general the wife and children should not be relegated to a significantly lower standard of living than that which the husband enjoys.
3. Subject to what follows, neither should the standard of living of the wife be put significantly higher than that of the husband, since to do so would amount in effect to imposing a fine on him for his matrimonial offence, and "that is not justified by the modern law."
4. In determining the relevant standard of living of each party, the courts take into account the inescapable expenses of each party, especially but not exclusively the expenses of earning an income and of maintaining any children.
5. If the wife is earning an income, or if she has what could in all the circumstances be considered a potential earning capacity, that must be taken into account in determining the relevant standards of living.
6. Where the wife is already earning an income, that ought generally to be brought into account, unless it would be reasonable to expect her to give up the source of income.
7. Where the wife is earning an income, the whole of this need not and should not ordinarily be brought into account so as to benefit the husband. This consideration is particularly potent where the wife only takes up employment in consequence of a disruption of the marriage

by the husband, or where she would not reasonably be expected to be working if the marriage had not been so disrupted.

8. At the end of its case, the court must ensure that the result of its order is not to press the husband below subsistence level.

Additional factors

In addition to those guidelines, judges consider the following:

1. the duration of the marriage and the number of children (if any);
2. the ages, health and occupational status of the spouses;
3. the extent of the property of the husband and how and when it was accumulated;
4. the extent of the property of the wife and how and when it was accumulated;
5. the income of the husband, and his potential future income from all sources;
6. the contribution of both spouses to the marriage, including financial and non-financial contributions.

We can see how judges consider and adapt these factors by examining one recent divorce case. (*Silverstein,* 1 RFL 2nd 239 Ont.) The parties had been married almost thirty-eight years. Mrs. Silverstein was sixty-two at the time of the divorce, Mr. Silverstein seventy.

At the time they met, in the 1930s, Mr. Silverstein, an immigrant from Poland, was a travelling salesman and Mrs. Silverstein was a secretary. They married in 1940, and in 1941 they opened a furniture store. The business was registered in Mr. Silverstein's name alone. The couple moved into the store, converting the back into temporary living quarters and then an upstairs apartment. After about three years, they bought a home and moved out of the store apartment.

In the 1940s, Mr. Silverstein bought another furniture store and an investment property. In the 1950s, he bought another investment property and, with a partner, incorporated a company to run his furniture business. There were more purchases, sales and consolidations throughout the 1950s and 1960s and by the time of the trial in 1978, Mr. Silverstein's net business worth was at least $400,000. In 1972, the couple had moved into a house worth at least $235,000.

The judge dealt with the property division first, and then the maintenance application under the Divorce Act. As a result of the property division, the wife ended up with assets having a total value of between $208,000 and $228,500. She had debts of about $24,700. The husband ended up with assets having a total value of $400,000 and debts of $40,000.

Mrs. Silverstein was not working and was in a poor state of health. The judge was satisfied she would not work in the future. Her annual income would be about $12,500 from investing her assets. (The judge assumed she would use a large portion of her assets to buy a condominium, the matrimonial home having been ordered sold.) Mr. Silverstein had high blood pressure and felt he wouldn't be able to work much longer. The judge was satisfied that he had an approximate annual income of $35,900, made up of salary, old-age pension, CPP, income from commercial property and income from invested proceeds.

Mrs. Silverstein presented a budget that would require a monthly after-tax income of $2,700, which she said would maintain her in the same standard as when she was living in the luxurious matrimonial home. The judge replied:

> While it is true that upon separation it is desirable that the non-income-producing spouse should not be relegated to a lower standard of living than that enjoyed by the spouses while living together, that standard can only be maintained after separation if there is sufficient earning capacity to maintain it. It is my view that [the wife's] demands are completely unrealistic.
>
> While there are some exceptions, for example, when one spouse has an exceptionally high earning capacity, it is usually the case upon separation that both spouses must expect to live at a lower standard of living than that enjoyed while they were living together. Usually there is not enough money available for both to live as well separately as they did when living together. In my opinion this applies to the Silversteins as to most other persons in their position. I think they both have to realize this simple though perhaps for Mrs. Silverstein, unfortunate fact of life. She will have to reduce her standard of living and her expectations as her husband has had to do.

He went on to say that in this case, what must be decisive in determining the amount of maintenance was the *means* of the parties. Given their respective incomes, he ordered the husband to pay the wife

$1,000 monthly. This would leave Mr. Silverstein with an annual income of $23,900 and Mrs. Silverstein with an annual income of $24,500. In doing this, the judge took into account the fact that Mr. Silverstein could and in fact might even be earning more than what was disclosed in the records of his company. (Mr. Silverstein did not produce at trial a book recording certain cash sales that his wife alleged would show a higher income than reported on the usual books. The judge said Mr. Silverstein could have produced the book to refute the allegations; since he had not done so, the judge said he was drawing inferences unfavourable to him.) In addition, Mr. Silverstein would have a tax benefit in that he could deduct the monthly payments, whereas Mrs. Silverstein would have to pay taxes on those payments.

When are wives ordered to pay maintenance?

There are a number of cases where wives are ordered to pay child maintenance. However, the number of reported cases where wives are ordered to pay maintenance to their husbands is small; these cases usually involve husbands in ill health.

In one case, a man and woman, aged about sixty years, were married for just over two years. Throughout this time, they lived entirely on the wife's income and assets. The husband had quit his job; the wife worked as a practical nurse. At the end of the marriage, the husband had a pension of $360 a month and a vacant lot worth $10,000. Because of his age and poor health, the judge found it unlikely he could return to full-time work. The wife had considerable assets and was still employed. The judge ordered a lump-sum payment to the husband of $12,000. (*Noble,* 16 RFL 368 B.C.)

In another case, the husband had founded two companies and, for tax reasons, made his wife the sole shareholder. She took legal and effective control when the companies were in difficulties. At the time of the divorce, the husband's health was seriously impaired and his income-earning ability very much in doubt. The wife was ordered to pay the husband a lump-sum payment of $25,000 *plus* $25,000 annually, payable as $2,080 monthly. The annual payment amounted to about one-third of the wife's annual income. In addition, there was about $100,000 of undistributed income in the company over which the wife had absolute control and which was available to her. (*Miller,* 6 RFL 2nd 252 Ont.)

In another, a paraplegic husband on welfare claimed maintenance. His wife, who was earning $9,100 annually, supported three children. Maintenance was refused. (*McLeod,* 2 RFL 386 Man.)

Is a maintenance claim affected by a delay between separation and the divorce hearing?

The longer you go without asking for financial support, the harder it will be to convince a judge that you need it at the time of divorce. Thus if you are separated for, say, nine years before initiating divorce proceedings and asking for maintenance, your chances of obtaining maintenance will be somewhat smaller than if you had asked at the time of the separation. Remember that you have the option of asking for support under provincial legislation before the divorce.

In one case, the parties separated in 1972, but only in answer to the husband's petition for divorce in 1976 did his wife ask for maintenance. Her husband then argued that if she could live without his help for those years, there was no reason why she could not continue to do so. But the judge was satisfied with her explanation: during those four years, she had been encroaching upon the capital she had received on the sale of the matrimonial home, and this, together with modest earnings from her employment and the assistance of friends and relatives, had permitted her to exist in a very frugal manner. Her assets were now depleted; she was unable to work and a public charge, so the situation was entirely different than in the first years of separation. The judge ordered maintenance. (*Szabo,* 5 RFL 2nd 176 Ont.)

When will a lump-sum payment be ordered?

Lump-sum payments are often preferable to periodic payments. There is no need to worry about collecting each month, about whether the respondent will move from the jurisdiction of the court or lose his job. And once the payment is made, there is no need for further contact. Finally, lump-sum payments are not taxable.

There are a number of situations where a lump-sum payment is considered more appropriate by judges than periodic payment, or warranted *in addition to* periodic payments. These have been developed as follows:

1. Where the respondent's assets are in a liquid form and permit painless separation of a lump sum. In other words, the respondent

does not have to sell property or shares to raise the payment.

2. Where the respondent is of advanced age.

3. Where the petitioner has demonstrated an ability to deal with a lump sum properly.

4. Where the parties are anxious to bring their relationship to a complete end.

5. Where the imposition of an obligation to pay periodic sums would create further conflict between the parties. In one case, a judge ordered a lump sum in view of "the patent animosity between the former spouses, which is attested to by the innumerable applications . . . to deal with, in an effort to bring this matter to a conclusion, the acerbity with which all proceedings in this case have been conducted, and the sheer weight and volume of the registry file. It is obvious that the less these two people have to do with each other from here on, the better for both of them. . . .' (*Reid,* 15 RFL 125 B.C.)

6. Where a lump sum is necessary to provide a home for the petitioner.

7. Where the history of the relations of the parties shows that the respondent has failed to meet periodic payments, and the only way to assume that the petitioner will be maintained is by a lump-sum payment.

8. To provide a nest egg against the contingencies of life.

9. To recognize the contribution of a spouse to the marriage. In one case, where a judge ordered periodic payments and a lump sum, he noted:

> The petitioner [wife] kept house, bore and raised the respondent's children, worked occasionally, but generally fulfilled her role as a wife and mother (although not apparently to the satisfaction of the respondent). She made a positive contribution to, and is entitled to a share of the matrimonial wealth that accumulated during the marriage. (*Cornish,* 2 RFL 2nd Nfld.)

In another case, a judge ordered a lump sum, saying:

> There was a contribution by the wife to the accumulation of assets of this marriage. She participated in the business to some extent, she did the books, she contributed earnings from part-time work during the course of the marriage, she did a considerable amount of work in mak-

> ing the home livable and effecting repairs and renovations to the marital home, which had been struck by lightning, so certainly there is a contribution to the marriage made by her. . . . (*Newman,* 4 RFL 2nd 97 N.S.)

This particular guideline is not as crucial where the previously discussed property reform legislation exists. As we noted, a wife will probably get a share of the property if she played the above role. But in those provinces and territories where there is no reform, it is still highly relevant.

10. To repay debts. In one case where a wife had borrowed $5,000 from her parents to help support herself and her children until the divorce trial, the husband was ordered to pay the wife $6,000 so that she could repay that debt. (*Gelgoot,* 1 RFL 2nd 204 Ont.)

None of the above factors are essential for the judge to order a lump-sum payment. But any one or more of them may mean that a lump-sum award is more likely.

There is no fixed rule as to what percentage of the husband's assets or net worth will be awarded as a lump-sum payment. In the past some judges have said that five or six percent would be awarded, but this rule no longer holds true.

In one case, the judge, after determining it would be more appropriate for a wife to get a lump-sum payment than periodic maintenance, did the following calculation to arrive at a figure: he estimated the wife, who was in her sixties, would need about $1,250 a month or $15,000 a year to maintain her former standard of living. In addition, she would need $6,000 a year for taxes and thus a gross income of $21,000 a year. He then estimated her own income from a pension and investments to be $15,950 a year. Thus there was a yearly deficiency of $5,050. The judge was informed by the wife's lawyer that, based on actuarial tables, the wife's life expectancy was approximately thirteen years. Consulting capitalized financial compound interest and annuity tables and assuming the interest rate was 8.75 percent, he awarded the wife a lump-sum payment of $40,000. This payment would yield the wife $5,050 a year with little or nothing left at the end of the thirteen years. (*Blackham,* 1 RFL 2nd 160 B.C.)

What effect do separation agreements have on maintenance orders? Often by the time the divorce is heard, the parties have already agreed what the maintenance payments will be. Usually the separation agreement, as it is called, will then be incorporated into the decree nisi and the terms will continue to apply. Sometimes, however, one of the parties is not satisfied with the agreement and wants the judge to consider the circumstances anew.

Increasingly, judges are taking the position that they have the right to do this regardless of the separation agreement and its terms. In one case, the parties had signed a separation agreement in 1973 when the husband was earning about $44,000 a year, whereby he paid his wife $1,400 monthly. By the time of the divorce hearing in 1976, he was earning $82,000 a year and his wife asked for a higher monthly payment. The judge said that, considering the "condition, means and other circumstances" *at the time of the trial,* the sum of $2,500 monthly would be more reasonable and so ordered. (*Derbyshire,* 30 RFL 173 Alta.)

This is not to say that separation agreements should be entered into lightly, or that their terms will automatically be overlooked. But the divorce court judge does have the power to order terms other than those in the agreement and in certain cases, where the husband or the wife asks him to do so, he will.

Judges are particularly likely to examine carefully the terms of the separation agreement when children are involved. Here they might interfere with the terms of a separation agreement that concerns child support even if neither the husband nor the wife asks them to do so. In one case where the separation agreement had not provided for any child support, the judge said:

> Parties to a separation agreement, assuming they are acting freely, are properly advised, and are of legal age to do so, are at liberty to waive or otherwise sign away any rights either may have with respect to the other, and this includes any right of support which a wife may have of her husband. However, infant children are not parties to any such agreement, and neither party has the right to waive or sign away inherent obligations which either may have toward those infant children. From the moment of birth, a child has an inherent right to support and maintenance from the parents, and the parents have an inherently continuing obligation to provide that support and maintenance until such time as that child is able to support and maintain itself. It is the duty of the court, I think, to scrutinize any separation agreement which touches

> upon the maintenance of children to ensure that they, as innocent third parties, are not prejudiced thereby.

In this case the judge ordered the father to pay $75 a month child support, even though the mother was not asking for it. (*MacKenzie,* 25 RFL 354 P.E.I.)

In another case, where a wife was on public assistance and no child support had been provided in the separation agreement, the divorce court judge ordered her husband, who earned $20,000 a year, to pay $125 a month for each of the four children. Here again the mother was not asking for child support, but the judge ordered it anyway, noting that "as between the state and the father surely the latter has a greater responsibility to those children." (*Manson,* 2 RFL 2nd 93 Alta.)

What arrangements can be made until the divorce is heard?
As discussed in chapter 3 on divorce, judges have the power to make interim orders to provide for support until the divorce hearing. Applications for interim support can be brought as soon as the divorce petition is issued. The judge can order whatever sum he thinks reasonable, having regard to the means and needs of the husband and wife. The judge, in looking at the needs of the parties, will only look at the short-term needs, i.e. how much is needed until trial. He will not take into account major expenses — for example, orthodontic work — that can be put off or that will probably not occur until after the divorce hearing. Thus the amount ordered on an interim basis is usually less than that ordered at trial.

In looking at the means of the parties, the judge will consider their income and assets. Only if a wife does not have the means to satisfy her needs until trial will she get interim support. If a wife has assets that produce an income sufficient to satisfy her needs until trial, her application for interim support will be dismissed. However, a wife is not expected to deplete her only capital asset to carry herself through to trial. Where a wife had only one asset, namely a $6,000 term deposit, the judge ordered her husband to pay her interim support, saying it would be unreasonable to expect the wife to deplete her capital to maintain herself until the trial. (*Tate,* 16 RFL 293 B.C.) In that case, the wife was not working because of health reasons, and other than her $6,000 term deposit, she had no income or assets whatsoever.

The judge may look at a wife's *potential* earnings. If she has worked in the past, but is not working at the time of the interim application, there will have to be convincing reasons, such as health, why she is not working. Otherwise, the judge will calculate in her means what she would be earning if she were in fact working.

When do payments begin and how long do they continue?

A judge has the power to order the maintenance payments to be paid retroactively from the time the divorce petition was issued, even if that was months or years before the final hearing.

Generally maintenance payments continue throughout the joint lives of the husband and wife. As soon as one or the other dies, the payments are no longer due. The judge can, however, order a different termination date. He can order the payments for only a certain period of time, or he can order that the payments be made for the lifetime of the wife. In the latter case, if the husband dies first, his estate will be liable for the payments. The judge can also order that child maintenance payments be made from the husband's estate.

The fact that a wife lives with another man or remarries does not automatically terminate divorce maintenance payments. Often, however, divorce judges explicitly order that the payments continue only until the wife's remarriage or cohabitation with another man.

Can the orders be changed if financial circumstances change?

The Divorce Act gives a judge the power to change any order he made "from time to time," if he thinks it fit and just to do so, having regard to the conduct of the parties since the making of the order or any change in the condition, means or other circumstances of either of them. But the terms of the divorce are not disturbed lightly, and there must be some material change in circumstances before a judge will vary a previous order. These circumstances might include a wife's inability to keep working, due to health or other reasons, increased expenses on the part of the wife, or increased income or assets on the part of the husband. The husband might bring an application to have the amount reduced if his income decreases, the wife's income or financial situation improves, or his expenses increase. The judge will weigh the various factors and make a determination. He will not go back to the original judgment to determine if it was correct, but will merely consider the situation at the time of the variation application, to see if there has been a material change in circumstances.

In one case, where a husband received a fairly substantial inheritance after the original divorce order, the judge increased the wife's monthly allowance maintenance payments because the husband would have significantly more income with the inheritance. (*Pruden,* 28 RFL 83 B.C.) The fact, however, that a husband receives a higher income in one year alone would not be considered enough of a change in circumstances to warrant a variation. If there is a significant and longer-term change in the circumstances, a variation may be ordered. For example, where a wife's income had remained the same since 1975, but her assets had depleted and her cost of living had significantly increased, the judge ordered the husband to pay more maintenance in 1978. The husband's income had increased substantially and his assets had not depleted. (*Walker,* 6 RFL 2nd 119 Ont.)

If a wife remarries, her husband may bring an application to vary the maintenance order. If it is demonstrated that his wife's financial situation has improved as a result of her remarriage, he will probably be successful in having the payments reduced or terminated. (If the divorce judgment said maintenance was only payable until the wife's remarriage, the husband will not even have to bring a variation application.) In one case where a woman remarried, her husband was also successful in having the amount of child maintenance reduced, because the financial circumstances of his former wife and his children had now improved. (*Kleiner,* 26 RFL 254 Ont.)

Where, however, a husband brought an application to have the amount of maintenance lowered because of his former wife's sexual behaviour after the divorce, it was refused. The court said: "A spouse's sexual misconduct is only one factor to be considered, financial considerations being of paramount importance. Only when the former affects the latter should a variation be warranted." (*Seeman,* 28 RFL 275 Ont.)

Child Support

You must always distinguish between financial support for a spouse and for children. Although a spouse may not get support, either because grounds do not exist in the "fault" provinces or because the judge does not think the finances and other considerations warrant it, child support will be denied only if the respondent is very impecunious. In those provinces where fault is not a criterion, either the husband or the wife may be ordered to pay child support. This is also true under the Divorce Act. And even in some of the "fault" provinces, such as New Brunswick, a mother can be ordered to pay support to the father for the child in his custody.

For how long must one pay child support?

The obligation for child support or maintenance varies from province to province. In Ontario and Prince Edward Island, each parent has an obligation to provide support to a child who is unmarried and under the age of eighteen years. If the child is sixteen or over, however, and has voluntarily withdrawn from parental control, the obligation ceases. In British Columbia, the obligation to pay child support continues to the age of nineteen years. Under the Divorce Act, a child is defined as a person under the age of sixteen years, or sixteen years of age or over, under his parents' charge "but unable, by reason of illness, disability or other cause to withdraw himself from their charge or provide himself with the necessaries of life."

In one divorce case where a twenty-year-old was attending an institute of technology for a three-year course in radiology, the judge ordered the father to pay maintenance for the "child" to the mother. He perceived the education as a "necessary of life" that the daughter was unable to provide for herself. (*Caryk,* 6 RFL 185 B.C.) In another, however, where a twenty-one-year-old, living with her mother and working part-time, had enrolled in college to obtain a degree in child care, the judge would not order maintenance. (*Neutce,* 30 RFL 16 B.C.)

Who will be ordered to pay support?

Often a spouse, even if not the natural parent of the child, will be ordered to pay support or maintenance. If he or she has treated the child as his or her own, most of the provincial laws as well as the Divorce Act will require support payments.

How much will be ordered?

Since, under the Divorce Act and many provincial acts, the obligation to maintain children is placed equally upon both parents, judges when determining the amount of child support take into account the relative abilities of both parents to discharge the obligation. A simple method of calculating the appropriate amount is to estimate the monthly cost of the child. The non-custodial parent is ordered to pay the custodial parent a part of the child's expenses proportionate to the relation his income bears to the total incomes of both parents. Thus if the total monthly cost of the child is estimated at $600, the non-custodial parent earns $20,000 yearly and the custodial parent $10,000, then the non-custodial parent, because his income is two-thirds the total, will be required to pay two-thirds the cost of the child, or $400.

There may of course be difficulties in calculating exactly how much a child costs — what portion of the rent or food is attributable to him or her; how much do clothes cost each month; how much is allowed for transportation and entertainment? There are no fixed answers to these questions, but at least some portion of the rent and food should be attributed to the child. Many cities and provinces have social planning councils or other groups that put out yearly statistics on the cost of raising a child at any particular age. These are usually minimum costs, but help as a basic guideline in trying to calculate the amounts.

Just as payments of spousal support are taxable if made on the basis of court order or written agreement, so also is child support. You should keep in mind when determining how much child support you will need that a portion of it will be taxed away.

There is no fixed figure of what is "proper" child support. You will often hear that $25 or $50 a week is the "going rate," but this is not reliable. Depending on the child's age, standard of living when the family was living together, extracurricular and special needs, and the parents' incomes and assets, the figure will vary from family to family.

7.
SEPARATION AGREEMENTS

Everyone who is separated is legally separated, in that no one can force you to live with a spouse you do not want to live with; there is nothing illegal about separating. True, certain implications follow from separation and as we have seen, sometimes one can be penalized, for example in custody matters, for initiating the separation. Separation agreements do not make separation "legal," they just tie up many loose ends that exist as a result: what will happen to the children? What will happen with the property, including the house, household goods, insurance, bank accounts? Will there be support payments and if so, how large?

Separation agreements try to settle these matters to the mutual satisfaction of the spouses. A separation agreement is simply a contract between a husband and wife, whereby each agrees to certain rights and obligations after the marriage breakdown. Like all contracts, they are arrived at through a series of negotiations, where each party puts forward what he or she wants and then accepts, varies or rejects the other party's proposals. As with all bargaining, each party often asks for more than he or she is willing to settle for, and a compromise is reached through negotiation. Since the final terms arrived at will govern the obligations of both for the future, each party must be realistic, not only about what he or she can live with in the present but also about his or her requirements in the future. Important items must not be given up lightly. As with all contracts, once you agree to a term in a separation agreement you are bound by it. It cannot be changed unilaterally.

Separation agreements do not require the sanction of a court. They are private contracts, entered into in the privacy of your lawyer's office, and they do not have to be presented to a judge for final approval. As we have seen there are certain items, for example support, that a judge might overlook if the agreement is ever brought into court. But this is more an exception than a rule. And even if a judge overlooks the clause relating to support, the other items in the agreement are still binding.

Do you need a separation agreement?

Nowhere in the law is a separation agreement required. If there are no outstanding issues to settle with your husband, no children and no support requested, a separation agreement is not necessary. If there are just a few items of household property to be divided or a house to be sold, and you and your husband have already agreed on this, it is unnecessary to incorporate those matters into a separation agreement. Neither is a separation agreement required if you are planning to get divorced in three years on the grounds of mutual separation. An agreement can be introduced as corroboration of the three-year separation, but there are other ways of proving that — friends, relatives, leases.

Sometimes even people with many outstanding disagreements, such as custody of the children, property division or support payments, do not wish to enter into an agreement. Sometimes they simply want to see how things go before putting anything in writing. This might work, although you should not bank too much on vague promises that cannot be enforced, and people often get less generous and more forgetful as time goes on. It is usually better to delineate the terms at the time they are discussed and supposedly agreed to, than to settle for a handshake. Rarely in the world of business is a deal settled this way. Although there is a myriad of emotional issues overhanging the marriage breakdown, separation agreements basically deal with financial matters and should be approached in as business-like a way as possible. You should not feel you are being crass or paranoid if you want to reduce an agreement to writing.

Often women feel pressured into signing agreements. They think it is better to take what their husbands offer than to go through the protracted and often unpleasant process of negotiating an agreement. Or often husbands will say: "If you do not take this, you will get nothing." In these cases, it is better if at all possible to stand back and let the matter ride for a while. Do not be pressured into signing an unsatisfactory agreement. It is not good practice to make any major decisions in a time of severe emotional stress, particularly decisions that will so fundamentally affect your future well-being. Try to treat the negotiation of separation agreements as you would the negotiation of any business or financial contract, like purchasing a house, signing an employment agreement, or selling a business. Remember that you always have the option of asserting your rights in court instead, but if you do not want a bitter court battle it is just as likely that your husband does not want one either. Do not be cajoled into signing a separation agreement simply out of fear of court proceedings.

Although many marital breakdowns end in the signing of a separation agreement, sometimes a court application is made first. Often wives feel they must prove they are serious about their claims for support; only when they initiate court applications will the other side believe them. Sometimes a husband does not realize how weak his position is until a court application is actually launched and proceeded with. But as we saw in chapter 3 on divorce, an agreement is often reached after the interim cross-examinations or orders, and the negotiation of less contentious items can proceed.

Sometimes the parties can agree on several items but have reached a stalemate on another. A decision then has to be made on whether to pursue that item in court or abandon it. This will depend largely on what you think of your chances in court. If, for example, your husband is offering $500 a month in support and you want $600, you will have to consider how likely it is that you would get the higher figure in court. Since no one can predict with accuracy what a judge will order, it is often better to accept the lower offer if the difference is small, particularly if you consider the court costs of fighting for the higher figure. In the end, you may gain nothing. Only if the figures are substantially different is it usually worth a fight.

Another matter you will have to consider when you are planning to reject an offer on a certain item is whether you will then be losing all the other items that have been tentatively agreed to. No one can be forced to sign an agreement, so your husband may say that he will retract the whole agreement if you do not accept $500 a month for support. If you are going to lose generous settlements on other items — perhaps insurance benefits or a cost-of-living index — and it seems unlikely that you could get anything as good in court, it may be to your overall benefit to accept the lower support offer in order to get the other settlements. Always look at the agreement as a whole package; don't become obsessed with one item.

What are the advantages of a separation agreement?

Avoiding court. Court battles are inevitably more costly and draining than the negotiation of separation agreements. Your lawyer will probably spend more time and therefore charge you more money to prepare a case for court than to negotiate a separation agreement. Often you will need expert witnesses for court hearings, and these cost money, too. In addition, courts are very formal places and people rarely feel relaxed there. Often they cannot express themselves the way they would like to. On the whole, the experience is seldom constructive. It usually ruins any remnants of good feelings that might have existed between a husband and wife. If there are children, the court experience will inevitably be harmful to the future relationship between the mother, father and children. This is not to say that you should be afraid of going to court, should it be necessary, but it is not something to relish.

Including your own terms. There are many items that parties might want to include in the separation agreement that a judge may not have either the power or the time to deal with. For example, many wives prefer to have their support payments tied to the cost of living, so that as the consumer price index rises, so do their support payments. Judges do not have the power to grant such an order. Or some parties want to have very complicated visiting schedules set out in the custody and access clause. Judges can often be impatient with such intricate arrangements and prefer not to order them.

Reducing taxes. If the parties have agreed to everything, and the husband is voluntarily paying his wife a monthly sum, it is preferable, at least for him, to put this voluntary arrangement in writing. Only if it is in writing is he allowed to deduct the payments from his taxable income. (Remember, however, that his wife then has to pay taxes on these payments.)

TERMS OF A SEPARATION AGREEMENT

Although there are standard separation agreements, just as there are standard leases, parties are free to vary, delete or add to these agreements as they see fit. A basic separation agreement is set out in the appendix to give you an idea of what they look like. But you do not need all these clauses, and you can add appropriate clauses for your own case.

Date of separation

An agreement will usually recite the fact that the separation has now been agreed to by both parties, and the date on which the separation took place. It may also, although not necessarily, indicate that the parties intend to live separate and apart for the rest of their lives.

Non-molestation, non-interference

Both parties generally agree not to interfere with each other in any way whatsoever.

Custody and access

If there are children, there will generally be a clause setting out the custody and access arrangements. The custody might be joint, or given to one party. The access might simply be "reasonable" or "generous" access or more specific, setting out the time, place and notice required for visits.

Support

If there is to be child support, the amounts will be set down, as well as the age at which payments will terminate. The support payable to the other spouse will be set out, including the date on which payments are to begin. These payments might be tied to the price index, or to an increase in the husband's salary. They might be graduated in such a way that a larger sum will be paid initially and decreasing amounts thereafter. There will usually be a clause whereby payments to a wife will stop when she remarries or begins living with another man in a husband-and-wife type of relationship. They might also terminate or decrease once the wife begins earning a certain salary. If there are young children, and it is likely that the wife will remarry or live with another man, then it is preferable to have a larger amount paid for the children's support and a smaller amount for the wife's. Then if she does remarry, the decrease in support won't seem that drastic. If the children are older, and the payments are only going to continue for a short time, it is better to have the larger amount payable to the wife, although again, if she remarries, that too will stop.

Variation clause

No matter what the change in circumstances, the terms of the separation agreement, like any contract, are binding. Because financial and other circumstances can change so significantly over time, many people like to have a vehicle in the agreement that allows renegotiation. This is often referred to as a "material change in circumstances" clause, and provides a procedure for renegotiation should one or both parties' circumstances change. If renegotiation is unsuccessful, the clause usually allows resort to arbitration or court determination. The material change in circumstances clause usually only relates to the custody, access and support provisions, leaving the other parts of the agreement intact.

Property division

The agreement usually sets out that personal property, including household goods, has been or will be divided in a certain way. It also provides for transfers of property such as the car or the house. In addition, it provides for division of property in the future. If the matrimonial home is not to be sold at present, it will set out who is to live in the house and for how long, and who is to pay its ongoing expenses. It will also set out the time and method of sale, and the division of proceeds.

Medical and hospital care

The agreement will often cover who is responsible and for how long for general medical and hospital care. It might also cover psychiatric and dental care, whether the husband or wife are to contribute to these expenses, and if so, in what proportion.

Insurance

Often wives are concerned about the finances of themselves and their children when the husband dies. There is frequently a clause whereby the husband acknowledges that he has or will obtain a certain amount of life insurance, and that his wife and/or children will be the irrevocable beneficiaries.

Other clauses

An agreement may also contain general release clauses, indicating that the terms of the agreement are the sole and final claims that the husband and wife will make against each other or each other's estates.

How long does the agreement last?

Because so much thought goes into negotiating and settling a separation agreement, parties like to know that it will last. Therefore there is usually a clause providing that even if there is a divorce later, the terms of the agreement will continue, meaning that the matters will not have to be relitigated at the time of the divorce. We saw that a judge does have the power in certain cases to disregard the agreement, but this power is rarely exercised. Merely entering into a separation agreement does not prevent either party from suing for divorce, on whatever grounds exist at the time or after the signing of the separation agreement. As long as the parties are married, sexual intercourse with another person gives rise to the grounds of adultery, even if the parties are separated and have entered into a separation agreement.

The fact that a wife commits adultery after entering into a separation agreement does not automatically mean that her support payments are stopped. Only if such a condition is written into the agreement will that happen. In Ontario, Prince Edward Island and British Columbia, "*dum casta* clauses" — as these provisions are called — are forbidden.

When is a separation agreement invalid?

The formalities of writing, signing and witnessing that the various provinces require for marriage contracts apply equally to separation agreements. And as with marriage contracts, if the agreement is entered into as a result of fraud or duress, or is unconscionable, it will be overlooked.

Fraud. An agreement is considered to be entered as a result of fraud if one party misrepresented a material fact and the other party entered into the agreement as a result of that misrepresentation. The deceived party may ask that the agreement be set aside on this basis. For example, a husband may have told his wife that he earned $20,000, and as a result of that she signed an agreement for a certain amount of support. If, after signing, she learns that in fact her husband earns $30,000 a year, the agreement can be overturned.

Unconscionable agreement. A judge will find unconscionable agreement where one side, through weakness or necessity, entered into an agreement that is clearly unfair or improvident. In one case, a woman who had fairly serious psychiatric problems became involved with a married man. The court found this was "a matter of grasping at anything which had the appearance of offering an alternative to a domestic situation which, for a number of reasons, including her own frailties, had become so distressing to her that she could not continue with it except at the risk of a further breakdown." (Some of the distressing circumstances were the habit her husband had of holding up a married woman friend as an example to his wife, asking why his wife could not be more like her, and telling his wife that she was "crazy" and threatening to return her to a psychiatric clinic.) She eventually told her husband she was going to leave "and go with the married man who told her he would take her away." She then agreed to sign documents that released her husband from any claim to support, turning over custody of all four children to him, and signing over her interest in the family home. For all this she was prepared to take $2,000, which she thought would give her a new start on life. The judge found she was making an improvident bargain. She was mentally competent but was, however,

> affected in her behaviour and her judgment and in such distress as to be subject to having advantage taken of her. She had had no business experience whatever. Her life had been made up of being a wife and mother and raising four of her husband's children. She did not know what her home was worth. I am satisfied her husband did; he had attended to all the family finances. She had never had a bank account.

The wife had signed the agreement without the advice of her own lawyer. The judge set the agreement aside, finding that she had

> shown marked inequality in the position of the parties, considering her circumstances of mental conflict and emotional upset, need, distress, dependence and relative ignorance, so that she was incapable of exercising proper judgment and protecting her interests. She has shown [us] also a substantially unfair bargain. (*Straiton,* 9, RFL 21 B.C.)

The finding of an "unconscionable" agreement is rare, and even rarer when each party has his or her own lawyer.

Duress. Finally, a judge might set aside an agreement signed under "duress or undue influence," such as violence, threats of violence or undue pressure. In one case, a wife had suffered a nervous breakdown and was hospitalized as a result of her husband's cruelty. Immediately upon her discharge from the hospital, the husband presented her with an agreement whereby he would give her $5,000 in return for her signing over all her property interests to him, which were worth about $60,000. The wife said she wanted to consult a lawyer, at which point her husband went into a rage and said he would give her $10,000. She then signed the agreement. The judge found there had been undue influence and set the agreement aside.

The setting aside of agreements is uncommon, and particularly so when lawyers are involved. When negotiating an agreement, therefore, it is not wise to believe that you will eventually be able to have it overturned. But these decisions do give some reassurance that if you have entered into a bad marriage contract or separation agreement, there might be a way out of it if one of the above three factors is present.

8.
STRATEGIES AND TACTICS

In earlier chapters, we have dealt with the substantive issues with which you will be concerned in marriage, separation and divorce. But none of these issues is resolved in a vacuum. There is always an encounter between two people, each often accompanied by a lawyer. And this encounter will not just take place in the context of courtrooms and legal proceedings. Marriage breakdowns are always very upsetting events to everyone involved, and they have an impact on many aspects of daily life.

Your lawyer will take care of the procedural matters — how and when to issue the petition requesting divorce; when, whether and how to conduct pre-trial discoveries; how to stage the trial. Your lawyer will also advise you on non-legal strategies: whether to empty out the joint bank account, whether to keep making purchases on your husband's charge cards. This advice will always take account of your particular situation — what the effects of your action might be, on what your husband and his lawyer might do and on how a judge might ultimately view it. For example, if you empty the joint bank account, this might discourage your husband from giving you financial support. On the other hand, it might encourage him to settle more quickly. It might convince a judge that you need less support, but on the other hand, it might show you are financially desperate and need more. Each case will be different, and only on consultation with your lawyer will you be able to decide any of these non-legal (not, we hope, *il*legal) strategies.

Along with their other aspects, marriages, separations and divorces have an element of business about them. As we've seen, they involve questions of incomes, property and jointly owned assets. When a marriage breakdown occurs, two people who may be used to thinking mainly about their joint interests each have to start thinking about their separate interests. And in many ways, there will now be a conflict between the interests of the husband and the wife. If, for instance, the wife feels that she should retain the matrimonial home, this is in conflict with the husband's interest, because he will be losing a portion of a valuable asset.

Very often in this situation, as in any bargaining situation between two people with different interests, one or both parties use tactics that are intended to get a better bargain for themselves at the expense of the other side. We accept this as normal in a business situation — say, between the buyer of a house and its seller, when each jockeys for the best possible deal. Although it is hard to accept that two people who have lived as a couple would deal with each other on such a basis, generally some use of bargaining strategies and tactics happens, to a greater or lesser extent, in a separation or divorce. Sometimes it is done consciously; at other times, unconsciously.

So you should be prepared for your husband's tactics. They may be worrying and upsetting; often this is exactly what is intended, in order to persuade you to resolve your outstanding differences by settling for less. All the time legal proceedings are underway, and even before they begin, you or your husband might be taking other actions. Although sometimes they are purely arbitrary or impulsive, malicious or vengeful, just as often they are calculated to force a particular response.

For example, in a non-matrimonial context like buying a house, you might delay putting your offer in to force the seller to take less. Your reason for the delay has nothing to do with any *personal* feelings you might have toward the seller (although, in fact, you might not like him). Rather it is to force a certain response on his part, namely a lowering of the price. Similarly, if you can look at your husband's and your own actions in that way, you will be better able to analyze what response is expected and how in fact you want to respond.

It is very common for husbands to engage in a variety of actions, all of which amount to economic blackmail, to encourage their wives to settle. Often a husband will cut off financial assistance to his wife. This might happen before separation; usually it happens shortly thereafter. He may not give her any money; he may close out the joint bank account; he may close all charge accounts; he may stop paying the house bills. You should not panic if any of these things happen. Often they have positive effects — they force you to take some action and not remain passive. Support applications can be brought very quickly, and in emergencies interim orders can be obtained almost immediately. Also, such actions by a husband create sympathy for the wife in the eyes of a judge, and cast the husband in a dishonourable light.

Similarly, you may find husbands who try to make their wives feel guilty or threaten them into settling. A common threat is that if the wife does not settle for what he is offering, the husband will oppose her request for custody of the children. Remember that a judge is going to look at what is in the best interests of the children in determining custody, however, not at how much or how little support the wife asked for. Or a husband may present himself as generous and considerate, and try to make his wife feel selfish. Here again, there are certain objective criteria a judge considers in determining financial support; the "generosity" of the husband is not one of them. You are best advised to ignore any such self-serving arguments on the part of your husband. You and your lawyer are your advocates now, not your husband.

Wives, too, often take certain actions to force their husbands into settlement. Some lock their husbands out, some clean out the joint bank account. Don't do this sort of thing without first discussing it with your lawyer. Locking your husband out might make him look like a pathetic victim, and cleaning out the joint bank account might make you look like a greedy wife.

Another category of actions on the part of your husband may be aimed at discouraging you from fighting at all, at embarrassing you and weakening your will. These may be in addition to the economic blackmail tactics. Usually husbands try to intimidate their wives by saying only *they* have all the facts and figures, only *they* know what it costs to live in the "real" world, only *they* know about investments and taxes. While such claims are usually false, even if they were true they should have no significance. The "facts and figures" will come out well before any court hearing, and the other items can be quickly learned if, indeed, the wife doesn't know them already.

As well as intimidating you, your husband may try to humiliate or embarrass you with certain allegations. You may be served with court papers that allege you have had extramarital affaires; that you are overemotional and hysterical; that you have neglected and ill-treated the children. These sorts of allegations are as common as white bread. Always remember they are *just* allegations, intended to bolster your husband's case and weaken you and your case. The judge will pay no heed to them unless they are proved. And even if they are proved, they must be relevant to the issue at hand. For example, if your application is for a division of family assets, an allegation that you are overemotional and hysterical has no relevance. Once you realize the allegations are set out for a strategic purpose — to weaken you — rather than taking them only as a personal affront, you will be better able to deal with such actions.

Often a husband will try to shock or hurt his wife, try to show how callous he can be. This may be an attempt to unnerve her. In one situation, a husband changed his will, striking out his wife as a beneficiary and replacing her with his present mate. He left a copy for the wife to see. Although these actions are initially upsetting, in the end they can be used against a husband — as evidence of his cruelty or his unreliability.

A more concrete class of actions are those the husband and/or wife take to change their real economic position. A husband frequently threatens to, and less frequently does, quit his job to avoid paying support. A judge does not have the power to force a husband to work; he does, however, have the power to order that the husband give his wife other assets: for example his half of the house, in lieu of support payments. Even a husband's threats to quit his job might persuade a judge that he is unreliable and that the wife should get certain assets as security. As with so many non-legal strategies, this too can be used against the husband. Often just before or during legal proceedings a husband will threaten to sell his assets and leave the country. A judge will be only too happy to give a restraining order, should that occur. In conjunction with court proceedings, a husband frequently undervalues his property, business and assets. He then appears to be worth less, and hopes that he will have to give his wife and children less. You can always have your own accountant or an appraiser put a value on your husband's assets. The two valuations together should give some objective standard of what the assets are really worth.

Another way a husband tries to change his real economic position is to go into debt between separation and the final court hearing. He will buy furniture for his new dwelling or a new car; he might even take on a second family. Part of the motivation for this may be to pay his wife and family less. Similarly, a wife often goes into debt between separation and a final court hearing (although this is often out of necessity, not calculation). Certainly the larger the debt, the more she needs. But be careful: there is a limit to what a judge will make a husband responsible for.

In the past, women might have questioned whether they should work outside of the home after separation, because of how this would affect the ultimate support order. This problem is now much less frequent. Most women who are able to work — either because of past experience or fewer responsibilities in the home — do in fact work, or hope to. They refuse to tie this fundamental question to the support issue. In any event, husbands no longer have a primary obligation to support their wives. Wives must now support themselves; only if they are unable to, may they turn to their husbands. Thus whether a wife should work is no longer as much a strategic question as a practical one. Does she have the training, can she afford child care, can she find a job?

You will find some lawyers who will encourage some or all of these tactics, some who discourage them. Always ask your lawyer why he or she is recommending a certain course of action. For example, he or she may be discouraging you from moving out of the matrimonial home. Is it to force your husband out? Is it so you will not lose custody? Is it, in the "fault" provinces, so you will not lose your right to support? Once you know the reason, you can make an informed decision about whether the pain is worth the result. You might also ask whether there are other ways of achieving the same result. Your lawyer is there to advise on strategy and tactics as well as legal rights and obligations. They tie into one another, and neither can be dealt with on its own.

CONCLUSION

We've now looked at the major issues women face in connection with marriage, separation and divorce. This should help to give you an idea of what you should think about when you approach these matters. As I said in the introduction, thinking about the possibility of marriage breakdown is never a very romantic thing to do, but it's an eventuality anyone can experience. Anyone thinking about or entering into a partnership of any kind — but particularly one you hope will last for a lifetime — should also think about what would happen if things fall apart.

As we've seen, there are still many areas where the law fails women, in spite of recent reforms in family law. It is true that divorces are easier to obtain than in the past. But women should not have to be subjected to the sort of cruelty we have seen in these pages in order to extricate themselves legally from a bad marriage. Several advisory groups and commissions have recommended "no-fault" divorce. That is, when a marriage is effectively over, these people say, there should be a simple legal remedy to end it. Whether the cause of the marriage breakdown is adultery, cruelty, homosexual acts or separation should be irrelevant; when the marriage is over, that should be all that counts. Rarely will you find one spouse saying the marriage has ended and the other denying it. Both usually admit its death, but because of the present laws they spend long and difficult hours — plus large amounts in legal fees — arguing about *why* it has happened. This may sometimes be useful in a therapeutic sense, but is it really an appropriate subject for laws, lawyers and judges?

You may have been surprised to find how limited and uncertain your property rights are. In most cases, you have no rights to your husband's assets while the marriage lasts. This seems unfair to women whose husbands could not be building up these assets were it not for the fact that their wives take on the majority of household duties, such as child care, housework and entertainment. And this is often done by women who also hold paid jobs outside the home. While this double workload might be recognized on marriage breakdown, is that enough? Some countries and some American states have implemented the doctrine of "community property," which means the assets of both spouses are shared throughout the marriage. Although this approach has its problems and in fact might not be what many women want, it does give you an idea of the possibilities for family property reform. Some people have suggested the community property approach, and thus immediate sharing, at least for property known as "family assets." The present system of deferred sharing often means that a woman cannot get credit, make her own investments, or set up on her own — at least not until her marriage is over.

But maybe the concept of sharing only in family assets, at whatever stage, is too limited. Does a woman's contribution to her family's welfare and wealth stop at the door of her home? Is it not somewhat artificial to divide the contributions made by each spouse by separating home activity from business activity? There is a legitimate worry that by setting up this division an incentive is created to keep assets away from the family and the home. If a husband knows his wife may eventually obtain half of the cottage, he might be tempted to invest his money in stocks, bonds and the like, which are strictly his. This certainly is an incentive for business, but is that really one of the means we want to use for priming the economy?

Even if you agree with the concept of dividing only family assets, and that only on marriage breakdown, the wide discretion given to the judges of all provinces to interfere with this division is disturbing. A wife does not know from the laws whether she will wind up with fifty percent of the family assets or any other property, and cannot know for certain until all litigation is completed. If the financial world were forced to operate at this level of uncertainty, the wheels of commerce would grind to a halt.

As we've seen, too, there are many problems with the legislated "equality" between husbands and wives and their obligations to support themselves. It is well known that on average, women's earnings are only sixty percent of men's earnings. Legal equality has not meant economic equality. But it is increasingly difficult for wives to get support from their husbands, even though a major cause of their problems in supporting themselves is this discrepancy in incomes. Until women's wages are equal to men's, until women get equal pay for work of equal value, no matter how long women work outside the home they will still need help from other sources. And of course, there are difficulties in collecting this support. Until the collection process is tightened up, a large portion of court orders will not even be worth the paper they are written on.

Family law has changed substantially over the last century and particularly over the last decade, in large measure because of political pressure brought to bear by women's organizations. But many more changes still have to be made before women are equals, legally and economically, with men in marriage and in divorce. Changes of this kind do not just happen; they come because women, as individuals and in groups and organizations, have recognized unfairness and inequity, and generated sufficient political pressure to overcome the vested interests in the status quo and to bring about reform. While we all should know our rights and our position under the laws as they stand, that knowledge underlines the need for many more reforms before we have truly fair and equitable laws in this country governing marriage, separation and divorce.

APPENDIX

Marriage Contract

THIS MARRIAGE CONTRACT dated this day of May, 1979:

B E T W E E N:

JOHN DOE , of the City of Toronto, in the Municipality of Metropolitan Toronto,

hereinafter called the "Husband"

who is the Party OF THE FIRST PART:

- and -

JANE DOE , of the City of Toronto, in the Municipality of Metropolitan Toronto,

hereinafter called the "Wife"

who is the Party OF THE SECOND PART:

both of whom are sometimes herein referred to as the "parties" or the "spouses", and each of whom as a "party" or a "spouse".

WITNESSES THAT:

WHEREAS the parties are a man and a woman about to be married on the 17th day of May, 1979 and this Agreement is made in contemplation of such marriage;

AND WHEREAS neither party has been married before or has any children or dependants and they do not intend to have any children;

AND WHEREAS it is the intention of the spouses to pursue individual careers during their marriage;

AND WHEREAS the parties now wish to resolve clearly and agree as to the ownership and sharing of diverse forms of property that may be owned by both or either of them during the marriage and provide for the orderly settlement of their affairs and their respective rights and obligations under the marriage, or upon separation, annulment, or dissolution of the marriage, or upon death, as particularly herein set out;

AND WHEREAS the parties believe that this contract

will bring certainty and confidence to their relationship to permit that relationship to encourage and strengthen their role as a couple in society;

NOW THEREFORE in consideration of the marriage, mutual love and affection, the premises and these presents and the mutual covenants herein contained, the spouses agree as follows:

1. APPLICABLE LAW:

(a) The proper law of this contract shall be the law of Ontario, and this contract shall also be deemed to be valid and enforceable in accordance with the law of any jurisdiction. The spouses intend all of their affairs and property to be governed by this contract and the law of Ontario.

(b) The spouses agree that the contract is valid and enforceable in Ontario and that they intend it to be a Domestic Contract in accordance with the Family Law Reform Act, 1978, and that it is legally binding.

(c) The spouses, while desiring this Agreement to operate both as a guideline to their marital rights and responsibilities and as a legally enforceable contract understand that some clauses of this Agreement may not be legally enforceable. Nonetheless, it is agreed that while the parties enter into this Agreement as a whole, they also agree to enter into each separate provision of this Agreement which is to be construed as a separate contract under ordinary contract law and enforceable as such.

2. LEGAL ADVICE AND DISCLOSURE: The parties acknowledge that each:

(a) Has received independent legal advice with respect to this contract;

(b) Understands his or her respective rights and obligations under the contract;

(c) Is signing this Agreement voluntarily.

3. MATRIMONIAL HOME:

(a) Ownership: The parties acknowledge that the house which they presently reside in at 40 Main Street, in the City of Toronto, in the Municipality of Metropolitan Toronto, is presently the sole property of the husband. The parties further agree that prior to the marriage of the parties, the husband shall transfer one-half of his interest in the said house to his wife in joint tenancy.

(b) **Sharing:** The home referred to in (a) above and any **subsequent matrimonial home which** is purchased by the parties shall not be considered a "family asset" for the purposes of the Family Law Reform Act.

(c) New Home: Notwithstanding the form in which title may be taken, the parties shall share ownership of the equity in any new matrimonial home in accordance with the proportions of their respective financial contributions to the acquisition, maintenance and capital improvement of such property.

(d) Matrimonial Home Contents: With the exception of those items set out in Schedule "A" which are the sole property of the wife, the spouses acknowledge that the household furnishings presently contained in the matrimonial home referred to in subparagraph (a) herein are the sole property of the husband.

4. PROPERTY REGIME:

(a) General: The spouses shall be completely separate as to property;

(b) Family Assets: The spouses agree that no property of either of them, either real or personal, shall be a "family asset" for the purpose of any division of interest therein pursuant to the Family Law Reform Act, 1978 or any successor or related or similar legislation.

(c) The spouses declare that each spouse shall be entitled absolutely without claim by the other to any property:

(i) owned by that spouse prior to the marriage;

(ii) acquired by that spouse solely after the marriage;

(iii) acquired by that spouse only by inheritance or third party gift at any time.

(d) Assets acquired after marriage: Each shall be entitled to share any assets jointly acquired after the marriage with each spouse's share solely determined by that spouse's financial contribution to the acquisition, maintenance, or capital improvement of the asset.

(e) Banking: It is the intention of the spouses to maintain separate banking accounts with each spouse being the sole owner of the monies in their accounts, free from any claim by the other spouse.

5. <u>SUPPORT</u>: The spouses acknowledge and agree as follows:

(a) The husband has a present annual income of $52,000.00 and the wife has a present annual income of $17,800.00 and both are presently self-supporting.

(b) The obligation of each spouse to provide support for himself or herself by remunerative employment prevails over the desirability of that spouse remaining at home to perform domestic or housekeeping duties.

(c) Subject to the terms of this Agreement, the sole obligation of support for a spouse is on that spouse and the other spouse shall not be called on to pay support to that spouse except as provided for in (d) herein.

(d) In the event of the separation of the parties, and if as a result of requests on the part of the husband there are adverse economic effects on the wife's career and income potential, it is agreed that:

(i) If separation occurs prior to May 17th, 1984

the husband shall pay to the wife a lump sum of $5,000.00.

(ii) If separation occurs on or after May 17th, 1984 but prior to May 17th, 1989, the husband shall pay to the wife the sum of $10,000.00.

(iii) If separation occurs on or after May 17th, 1989, the husband shall pay to the wife the sum of $15,000.00.

(e) If no agreement can be reached within thirty (30) clear days after the date of the separation as to whether or not a lump sum payment is owing to the wife, then such matter may be determined at the instance of either the husband or the wife, either:

(i) Under the Arbitrations statute then in force in a jurisdiction in which both parties reside, or in the Province of Ontario, this section 5(e)(i) constitutes a submission under such Arbitrations statute. After the said period of thirty (30) days' notice has expired without settlement of the said matter the husband and the wife shall have a further period of ten days in which to agree upon a single arbitrator and failing such agreement each shall have a further period of five days in which each may choose an arbitrator and the arbitrators so chosen by the husband and the wife shall chose a third arbitrator and the decision of a majority of such arbitrators shall be final, binding and conclusive upon the parties hereto. Such arbitrator or majority of arbitrators as the case may be shall further be entitled to award the costs of the application, but should not do so except in unusual circumstances; or

(ii) in preference to (i), before a Court having jurisdiction and the same power to make the said order for a lump sum payment as an arbitrator or panel of three arbitrators would have under the process described in section 5(e)(i) preceding including jurisdiction under the Divorce Act (Canada) or The Family Law Reform Act (Ontario) or similar or successor legislation in force from time to time in the permitted jurisdiction for the application and for this purpose the parties hereby confirm the jurisdiction for arbitration as in section 5(e)(i) above of any such court, as though in making the said order such court were with authority making one of its own orders.

(f) Aside from the possible obligation for the payment of a lump sum as provided for in 5(d) herein each spouse will remain solely responsible for his or her spouse's support and releases the other from any and all claims and causes of action for maintenance, support, interim maintenance, or interim support, and without limiting the generality of the foregoing, each party releases the other from any such claims under Part 2 of the Family Law Reform Act, 1978 (Ontario), and the Divorce Act (Canada).

6. <u>LIVING EXPENSES</u>:

(a) The spouses agree that they will each contribute to the joint household and ordinary living expenses in a manner proportionate to their incomes.

(b) Notwithstanding the provisions of subparagraph (a) neither party shall have the right to reclaim from the other party the amount of any excessive contribution to household expenses unless a contrary intention existed between the parties at the time of such excess contribution.

(c) The spouses agree that they will pay for their own personal expenses apart from joint household and living expenses.

(d) The spouses acknowledge that if the wife is working the parties shall employ a housekeeper every two weeks to assist in cleaning and maintaining the house.

(e) The cost of carrying the mortgage referred to in paragraph 3(a) herein will be the sole responsibility of the wife but will be considered as part of the household and ordinary living expenses for purposes of computation referred to in subparagraph (a) herein.

7. CHILDREN: The parties hereby agree to be mutually responsible for the care, upbringing and financial support of each child of the marriage. If the parties are unable to agree on separation with respect to the custody, access and support arrangements for any child or children of the marriage, such matters shall be decided in accordance with the terms of The Family Law Reform Act, as amended from time to time.

8. FINANCIAL DISCLOSURE: In order to carry out the provisions of paragraph 6 (a), the parties shall from time to time provide each other with such reasonable evidence of their monthly earnings as each may require.

9. DEBTS AND OBLIGATIONS:

(a) Neither the husband nor the wife shall contract in the name of the other, nor in any way bind the other for any present or future debts or obligations.

(b) The spouses agree that they shall not be obliged to pay or contribute to the payment of the present or future incurred debts of the other.

(c) If debts or obligations are incurred by the husband or the wife before or after the date of the execution of this contract, he or she shall indemnify and save harmless the other.

10. LIFE INSURANCE: The husband and wife represent and warrant that each will maintain the other as the beneficiary of any policies of life insurance or pension plan or any substitute or successor policy thereto while the parties are cohabiting as husband and wife. It is expressly agreed that if a spouse is named as beneficiary that he or she will not be designated as a beneficiary irrevocably.

11. ESTATES:

(a) While the parties are cohabiting as husband and wife, each of the spouses obliges himself or herself to make the other the sole beneficiary of his or her estate and each spouse will immediately effect a will valid for these purposes at death. This obligation shall cease on the parties ceasing to cohabit as husband and wife and the parties agree that they may then dispose of their estate by will in any manner whatever free from any claim of the surviving party.

(b) Subject to the requirement contained in (a) herein, the spouses release each other from all claims and rights which he or she may have or may afterwards acquire in the estate of the other upon the other dying intestate, whether by way of statutory allowance or right under the laws of any jurisdiction and in particular Part 2 of the Succession Law Reform Act, 1977 in force from time to time in the Province of Ontario and upon the death of the other, under the laws of any jurisdiction and in particular, Part 5 of the Succession Law Reform Act, 1977 in force from time to time in the Province of Ontario, and to act as executor or administrator of the other's will or estate.

12. RELEASE: The husband and wife each accept the terms of this Agreement in satisfaction of all claims and causes of action which each now has or may hereafter acquire in any manner including but not limited to Parts I, II and III of The Family Law Reform Act, 1978 and the Divorce Act (Canada) and including the Succession Law Reform Act, 1977 for possession of or title to or administration or executorship of property or support from the other whether before or after the death of the other and any claims whether arising out of the marriage of the husband and the wife or otherwise, except for:

(a) Claims arising under or to enforce the provisions of this contract; or
(b) Dissolution, simplicitor of the marriage;
(c) Claims and negligence for personal injury or property damage.

13. DIVORCE: If either the husband or the wife obtain a decree of divorce, all the terms of this Agreement shall survive and continue in full force and effect.

14. OTHER DOCUMENTS: Each party shall at any time and from time to time furnish or execute and deliver to the other party, any document or documents that the other reasonably requires to give effect to the terms of this Agreement.

15. <u>AMENDMENT</u>: The parties may amend any of the terms hereof by writing and signed by them and witnessed and endorsed on these articles.

16. <u>TERMINATION</u>: This Agreement cannot be terminated at any time except by written agreement of the parties.

17. <u>BINDING NATURE OF CONTRACT</u>: This contract shall enure to the benefit of and shall be binding upon the parties and their heirs, administrators, executors and assigns.

AND WITNESSES that in accordance with the terms herein the husband has executed this Agreement, setting hereto his hand and seal.

In the presence of:)

________________________) ________________________

AND WITNESSES that in accordance with the terms herein the wife has executed this Agreement, setting hereto her hand and seal.

In the presence of:)

________________________) ________________________

SCHEDULE "A"

2 chesterfields

2 armchairs

1 double bed

2 chest of drawers

1 complete dinner set

1 patio set

6 table lamps

4 carpets 9 x 12

bedding & linen

drapes

personal items

Petition for Divorce

Petition for Divorce

DYE & DURHAM CO. LIMITED
Form No. 817 - 824

Registrar's File No. D 19

In the Supreme Court of Ontario

Between

JANE DOE

PETITIONER

and

JOHN DOE

RESPONDENT(S)

PETITION FOR DIVORCE

(To be completed according to Form 140 as the same appears in the Rules of Practice)

To this Honourable Court:

See Form 140. **I hereby petition for a decree of divorce from the Respondent spouse** JOHN DOE and for custody of and maintenance for the children named in paragraph 6C, interim custody and interim maintenance for the said children, interim maintenance and permanent maintenance for myself, and costs, on a solicitor and client basis.

on the grounds and in the circumstances following:

1. GROUNDS:

See Form 140. **A. My Petition is under the DIVORCE ACT (Canada), section** 3 **, subsection** (d)

See Form 140. **B. The particulars of my grounds for divorce are:**

Since the celebration of the marriage, the Respondent has treated me with physical and mental cruelty of such a kind as to render our continued cohabitation intolerable, particulars of which are as follows:

1. The Respondent drinks to excess causing me pain, suffering, humiliation and embarassment:

(see pages 1a and 1b annexed)

Use additional page if necessary.

pg. 1a

(a) when I was in the hospital having given birth to our first child, the Respondent would visit me so drunk the other mothers in my room would comment on his state and question me about him.

(b) the Respondent so often came home drunk and abusive that when we were living on Main Street the owners who lived downstairs requested that we move because of the noise and disruption.

(c) on one Christmas Eve when the Respondent was drunk, we were visiting friends with our daughter Janie. The Respondent, in a rage, flung Janie by the arm out into the hall and closed the door behind her. Janie was screaming, crying and in a very upset and agitated state. Finally, our friends had to take the Respondent home, he was so drunk.

2. The Respondent has shown little respect for my intelligence, making me feel inadequate and unimportant. Often, in discussions with friends or relatives, the Respondent would tell me to 'shut up', that 'I didn't know what I was talking about'. These statements would embarrass me immensely.

3. The Respondent would frequently stay out until all hours of the night, not telling me where he was or when he would be home:

(a) often he would return home at 3 or 4 a.m. in the morning so drunk that when he would come to bed I would have to leave as he was so revolting. On a number of occasions he would come home very late and drunk with one of his male friends and they would both sleep in our bed. Once again I would have to leave the bedroom.

(b) when I started to have labour pains with the impending birth of my second daughter, it was 2 a.m., the Respondent was not home and I had no idea where he was. I had to take an ambulance to the hospital alone. The ambulance crew took my older daughter to a friend's apartment. The next morning I had the baby; the nurse called our apartment and the Respondent was asleep in the living room. He had come home, fallen asleep in the living room and did not even know that my daughter and I were not there.

4. The Respondent neglected me and the family and did not participate in household activities or chores:

(a) often the Respondent would not eat with me and the children; nor would he help me in feeding the children, dressing or bathing them.

page 1b

(b) when the Respondent took the children out for a drive, instead of taking them to a park or other outing, he would take them to a friend's house where he would just sit and drink; then he would drive home with them drunk.

5. The Respondent assaulted me physically on a number of occasions:

(a) once when we were having dinner and got into a slight disagreement,before I knew it the Respondent harshly slapped me across the face. I was so upset by this incident I cried and vomitted.

(b) one night when I was pregnant with my first daughter, the Respondent wanted to have sex. I was not feeling well and did not want to. The Respondent grabbed me around the neck and started to strangle me, and then pushed me to the floor.

(c) one month after I had our second child, the Respondent **got angry with me, rushed at me with the baby chair and hit me over the head while I was holding the baby in my lap. He then twisted my jaw. The children witnessed this incident and started crying and screaming.**

6. The Respondent's conduct toward me and the children has caused me nervouness, anxiety, and nausea for which I have had to seek medical treatment.

7. I have seen my family physician and a psychotherapist in the hopes of re-building my self-confidence.

8. As a consequence of the conduct described above, continued cohabitation with the Respondent became intolerable and I left the matrimonial home on or about September 5, 1978.

Page 2—Petition for Divorce
Dye & Durham Co. Limited, No. 818

2. RECONCILIATION:

A. The particulars of the circumstances which may assist the Court in ascertaining whether there is a possibility of reconciliation or resumption of cohabitation are:

1. The particulars outlined in paragraph 1 B above.

2. I do not wish a reconciliation with the Respondent.

State "no efforts to reconcile have been made" if such be the case.

B. The following efforts to reconcile have been made:

No efforts to reconcile have been made.

Page 3—Petition for Divorce *(Amended Sept. 1970)*
Dye & Durham Co. Limited, No. 819

3. PARTICULARS OF MARRIAGE:

(Where possible, set out the particulars from the marriage certificate)

A. The date of the marriage was: August 10, 1970

B. The place of the marriage was: Ottawa, Ontario

C. The surname of the wife before marriage was: Deer

D. The maiden surname of the wife was: Deer

E. The marital status of the spouses at the time of the marriage was,

wife: spinster **husband:** bachelor

F. The wife was born at Ontario (province or country) **on** June 14 (month, day) **19**43

G. The husband was born at Alberta (province or country) **on** January 7 (month, day) **19**40

Where such certificate cannot be produced substitute *"I am unable to file a certificate of the marriage or of the registration thereof because ...."*

H. Filed herewith is a certificate of the marriage or of the registration thereof.

4. DOMICILE AND JURISDICTION

(Street address need not be shown in A and B below)

A. My residence is in the municipality of Metropolitan Toronto

in the Province of Ontario

B. My spouse's residence is in the municipality of Metropolitan Toronto

in the Province of Ontario

C. I ceased to cohabit with my spouse on or about: September 5, 1978

D. My domicile is: Canada (Ontario)

E. Such domicile has subsisted since: birth

See Form 140.

F. I have **been ordinarily resident in the Province of Ontario for a period of at least one year immediately preceding the presentation of this Petition and actually resided in the said province for at least ten months of that period at** Toronto, the exact address of which is known to my solicitor.

Set out place or places of residence.

5. AGE AND DISABILITY

State *"No party to these proceedings is under 18 years of age"* if such be the case.

A. The names of any of the parties under 18 years of age and the ages of such parties are:

No party to these proceedings is under 18 years of age.

State *"No party to these proceedings is under any other legal disability"* if such be the case.

B. The names of the parties suffering any other legal disability and the nature thereof are:

No party to these proceedings is under any other legal disability.

6. CHILDREN:

State "there are no such children of the marriage" if such be the case.

A. The names and dates of birth of all living children of the marriage as defined by the DIVORCE ACT (Canada) are:

Janie Doe, born November 3, 1972, and Johnny Doe, born April 18, 1975.

State "not applicable" where no children are shown in para. A.

B. The particulars of the past, present and proposed custody, care, upbringing and education of the said child(ren) are as follows:

1. At all times since the separation, the children have resided in my custody and under my care and control.
2. I live in assisted housing with the children which has adequate room for the children and myself.
3. The children attend school in the neighbourhood.
4. I propose that custody of the children be given to me and that they continue to reside with me in the loving and secure home which I can provide for them.

State "not applicable" where no children are shown in para. A, or "no claim for custody is being made" if such be the case.

C. I claim custody of the following child(ren):

Janie Doe and Johnny Doe

State "not applicable" if no claim for custody is being made.

D. The facts on which such claim for custody is founded are:

1. I am willing and able to provide a secure and loving home for the said children and with the financial assistance of the Respondent to see to their material and educational needs, and to give them the parental care and direction they require.
2. The children are very young and require the care and attention which I can and am willing to devote to them. The Respondent has never shown that he is able or willing to devote any time to the children.
3. The Respondent has frequently displayed a violent temper in front of the children. This has had a detrimental effect on Janie who is a very nervous and anxious child and requires extra care and attention at this point.
4. I have taken the primary responsibility in raising the children. The Respondent's attention to the children has been inconsistent and negligible.

Use additional page if necessary

Page 5—Petition for Divorce *(Amended Feb. 1974)*
Dye & Durham Co. Limited, No. 821

7. OTHER PROCEEDINGS:

State "there have been no such petitions or proceedings instituted" if such be the case.

A. The particulars and status of all other petitions or proceedings instituted with reference to the marriage or any child thereof, including applications to the Parliament of Canada or actions for alimony or applications under any statute, and including any arrears of payments thereunder, are:

There have been no such petitions or proceedings instituted.

8. SEPARATION AGREEMENTS AND FINANCIAL ARRANGEMENTS:

State "there have been no such written or oral agreements between the parties" if such be the case.

A. The dates of any written or oral separation or financial agreements between the parties are:

There have been no such written or oral agreements between the parties.

Complete where a claim for corollary relief is made or state "not applicable" if no such claim is made.

B. The financial position, both income and capital, of the respective spouses is:

1. I am presently on welfare and receive the sum of $330.00 monthly. I intend to take a typing course and then to supplement my income by typing and babysitting. I have a one-half share in the matrimonial home.

2. The Respondent is an insurance adjuster with Great West Life. He earns a gross income of approximately $22,000.00 annually. He has a one-half interest in the matrimonial home and a 1977 Thunderbird worth approximately $6,000.00. I do not know what other assets he has.

9. COLLUSION, CONDONATION AND CONNIVANCE:

A. There has been no collusion in relation to this Petition.

Where the facts are otherwise, see Form 140.

B. There has been no condonation of or connivance at the grounds for divorce set forth in this Petition.

Page 6—Petition for Divorce *(Amended Sept. 1978)*
Dye & Durham Co. Limited, No. 822

10. JOINDER OF OTHER CAUSES OF ACTION:

When any other cause of action is joined with a matrimonial causes action, set out concisely in convenient following numbered paragraphs a statement of material facts relied upon:

Page 7—Petition for Divorce *(Amended Sept. 1978)*
Dye & Durham Co. Limited, No. 823

11. RELIEF ASKED:

I therefore ask this Honourable Court for the following relief:

A. A decree that I be divorced from the respondent, JOHN DOE:

B. custody of the children of the marriage;

C. maintenance for the said children;
D. interim custody of the said children;
E. interim support for the said children;
F. maintenance for myself;
G. interim maintenance for myself;
H. interim disbursements;
I. costs on a solicitor and client basis;
J. such further and other relief as this Honourable Court deems just.

12. DECLARATION OF PETITIONER:

I have read and understand this Petition. Those statements contained therein of which I have personal knowledge are true, and those of which I do not have personal knowledge I believe to be true.

DATED at Toronto , **this** 24th **day of** September , **19** 78.

JANE DOE (signature of petitioner)
c/o Cornish, King & Sachs
111 Richmond Street West
Suite 320 (address for service)
Toronto, Ontario
M5H 3N6

PLACE OF HEARING

* Insert *"Matrimonial Causes Sittings"* or *"High Court Sittings"* as the case may be.
See Rule 245, 775f and 799.

I propose that this Petition be heard at Toronto

at a* High Court Sittings **of this Court.**

STATEMENT OF SOLICITOR

See Form 140.

I, LYNN KING the solicitor for JANE DOE , the Petitioner herein certify to this Court that I have complied with the requirements of section 7 of the DIVORCE ACT (Canada).

DATED at Toronto , this 24th day of September , 19 78

(signature of solicitor)

Separation Agreement

THIS SEPARATION AGREEMENT made May 19, 197 .

B E T W E E N :

JANE DOE

- and -

JOHN DOE

WITNESSES:

The parties were married to each other in the City of Toronto, in the Province of Ontario, on February 10th, 1964. Throughout this Agreement they are called respectively the "husband" and the "wife", or in the case of a reference to the children the "father" and the "mother". In the event that the marriage is dissolved the terms shall be construed to mean "former husband" and "former wife". The husband and wife have three children: Sandra Doe, born April 5th, 1965; Mary Doe, born May 4th, 1967; Jack Doe, born June 2nd, 1969; all of whom are collectively called the "children" throughout, and each of whom is individually called the "child" throughout.

As a result of irreconcilable differences between them, the husband and the wife have been living separate and apart since May 13th, 1978, and each of them desires to settle by agreement all rights, claims, demands and causes of action which each has or may have against the other with respect to the custody, care and upbringing of the children, and with respect to their property, and with respect to any rights either or each of them has, or may have to support, or maintenance from the other.

THEREFORE, the husband and wife agree and acknowledge as follows:

1. LIVING SEPARATE AND APART: The husband and wife will continue to live separate and apart from each other for the rest of their lives.

2. FREEDOM FROM THE OTHER: Neither the husband nor wife shall molest, annoy or in any way interfere with the other or use any means to compel, or attempt to compel, the other to cohabit or live with him or her.

3. CUSTODY: The mother shall have sole custody, care and control of the children.

4. ACCESS:

(1) The father shall have access,

(a) every other weekend from Friday at 7:00 p.m. until Sunday at 6:00 p.m., provided that forty-eight (48) hours notice will be given if such access is not to be exercised;

(b) two weeks in the summer, provided that the father gives the mother one (1) months' notice in advance which two weeks such visit will take place;

(c) part of the Christmas holidays, one parent having the children from 3:00 p.m. Christmas Eve until 3:00 p.m. Christmas Day; the other parent having the children from 3:00 p.m. Christmas Day throughout Boxing Day, and the parties will divide the balance of the Christmas Holiday equally;

(d) alternate Thanksgivings.

(2) The father shall exercise his right to access outside the children's home and shall make all necessary transportation arrangements to collect the children and return them later to their home.

(3) The father shall not have access where it might reasonably be detrimental to the children's health or well-being.

(4) Neither the father nor the mother may remove the children from the Province of Ontario without the consent in writing of the other.

5. FINANCIAL SUPPORT: On December 1st, 1978, and on the first day of each month following, during the joint lives of the husband and wife, the husband shall pay to the wife,

(a) the sum of $300.00 for her own support until she remarries or lives with a man as if she had remarried; and

(b) $100.00 for each child for maintenance of that child (making a total of $300.00 for three children) until one or more of the following occurs,

(i) the child becomes 18 years old and ceases to be in full-time attendance at an educational institution;

(ii) the child ceases to reside with the wife;

(iii) the child becomes 21 years old;

(iv) the child marries; or

(v) the child dies.

6. MATERIAL CHANGE IN CIRCUMSTANCES:

(1) The husband and wife intend paragraphs 3, 4 and 5 of this Agreement to be final except for variation by reason of a material change in circumstances.

(2) Obligations arising out of the remarriage of the husband or of the wife or both are to be taken into account in determining whether there has been a material change in circumstances.

(3) If a material change in circumstances takes place, only the provisions in paragraphs 3, 4 and 5 of this Agreement may be varied.

(4) The husband or wife wanting the variation shall give to the other a notice of the variation he or she is seeking and the husband and wife may then confer with each other either personally or through their respective solicitors to settle what, if any, variation should be made.

(5) If no agreement has been reached thirty clear days after notice has been given under paragraph 6(4), variation,

(a) relating to:

(i) custody of the children;

(ii) access to the children;

(iii) maintenance of the children;

is to be determined upon application by either the husband or the wife under the relevant Act in force from time to time in the Province of Ontario.

(b) relating to alimony or maintenance for the wife is is to be determined at the instance of either the husband or the wife under The Arbitrations Act in force from time to time in the Province of Ontario through a single arbitrator whose award is subject to appeal to a Judge in Court and from a Judge in Court to the Court of Appeal.

(6) Paragraph 6(5) constitutes a submission under The Arbitrations Act in force from time to time in the Province of Ontario.

(7) The terms of this Agreement are to be final, except as varied under paragraphs 6(4) or 6(5) above.

(8) The right of variation for maintenance of the wife and maintenance of each child includes the right to forgive all or part of arrears that may have accumulated.

7. HEALTH AND MEDICAL EXPENSES:

(1) The husband warrants that he is maintaining in force for the benefit of the wife and children a plan issued by the Ontario Health Insurance Plan.

(2) The husband agrees to continue this plan or an equivalent plan for the benefit of the wife and children as long as he is required to provide for support of the wife and children under paragraph 5 of this Agreement.

(3) If the husband fails to maintain this plan of insurance, he is responsible for all hospital and medical expenses incurred by or on behalf of the wife or the children as long as he is required to provide for the support of the wife and children under paragraph 5 of this Agreement.

8. LIFE INSURANCE:

(1) The husband shall immediately deliver to the wife the three existing pollicies of insurance on his life totalling $100,000.00 in face value and consisting of:

(a) policy number 007 of World Insurance Company having a face value of $50,000.00;

(b) policy number 1008 of World Insurance Company having a face value of $25,000.00.; and

(c) policy number 1123 of The Universe Insurance Company having a face value of $25,000.00.

(2) The husband shall irrevocably designate the wife as beneficiary of these policies under The Insurance Act of Ontario.

(3) The husband agrees to maintain these policies of insurance for the benefit of the wife during her lifetime and shall pay the premiums on each policy of insurance as each falls due until maturity of each policy.

(4) If the wife
- (a) remarries, or
- (b) lives with a man as if she had remarried, or
- (c) dies before the husband,

the husband may deal with the policies of insurance as he deems fit free from any claim by the wife or her estate and the wife shall give any consent required to enable the husband to deal with these policies.

(5) The husband shall deliver a receipt to the wife not later than fourteen clear days following the date of payment of each premium under these policies and if the husband defaults in payment of the premium the wife may pay it and recover the amount of it from the husband together with all costs and expenses in so doing including the costs of her solicitor as between a solicitor and his own client.

9. PERSONAL PROPERTY: The husband and wife each acknowledge that:
- (a) all their personal property has been divided between them to their mutual satisfaction;
- (b) each is entitled to the personal property now in his or her possession free from any claim by the other; and,
- (c) each may dispose of the personal property now possessed by him or her as if he or she were unmarried.

10. MATRIMONIAL HOME:

(1) The husband and wife acknowledge that the house and lot municipally known as 100 Main Street in the City of Toronto is a family asset and each agrees that the house and lot are to be sold and the net proceeds equally divided between them.

(2) To minimize disruption to the children's schooling, the

husband shall permit the wife and the children to remain in exclusive possession of the house and lot without payment of occupation rent until June 30th, 1979, and any terms for sale are to contain and be subject to this right of possession.

(3) The husband and wife are to agree on the method of sale and division of the proceeds, but if they are unable to reach agreement before June 30th, 1979, sale and division are to be determined upon application by either husband or wife under The Family Law Reform Act, 1978.

(4) Upon application under paragraph 10(3), neither husband or wife shall assert against the other any right that he or she may have had to remain in possession of the house and lot.

(5) Upon division of the sale proceeds, all necessary accounts are to be taken and adjustments made so that from the date of separation until the date of sale, both husband and wife are to bear equally all charges relating to the house and lot including but not limited to mortgage payments, taxes, insurance premiums, expenses in maintaining the house and lot, and all expenses of sale.

11. DEBTS AND OBLIGATIONS:

(1) Neither the husband nor the wife shall contract in the name of the other nor in any way bind the other for any debts or obligations.

(2) If debts or obligations are incurred by the husband or the wife on behalf of the other before or after the date of this Agreement, he or she shall indemnify the other from all

(a) claims;

(b) costs;

(c) expenses;

(d) damages; and,

(e) actions,

arising from those debts or obligations.

12. RELEASE OF RIGHTS IN EACH OTHER'S ESTATE: The husband and wife release each other from all claims and rights that he or she may have had, or afterwards may acquire,

(a) in the estate of the other upon the other dying intestate, whether by way of statutory allowance or right under the laws of any jurisdiction and in particular The Devolution of Estates Act in force from time to time in the Province of Ontario;

(b) upon the death of the other, under the laws of any jurisdiction and in particular The Succession Law Reform Act in force from time to time in the Province of Ontario; and

(c) to act as executor or administrator of the other's will or estate.

13. RELEASE:

(1) The husband and the wife each accept the terms of this Agreement in satisfaction of all claims and causes of action each now has except for claims and causes of action

(a) arising under this Agreement; or

(b) for a decree of divorce,

including but not limited to claims and causes of action for custody, child-maintenance, alimony, maintenance, interim alimony, possession of or title to property, and any other claims arising out of the marriage of the husband and the wife.

(2) Nothing in this Agreement constitutes a bar to any action or proceeding of either the husband or the wife to enforce any of the terms of this Agreement.

14. NON-CONDONATION AND SEPARATION AGREEMENT TO SURVIVE DIVORCE: Nothing in this Agreement shall constitute a condonation by either spouse of any conduct or circumstances which but for this Agreement would entitle either spouse to a decree of divorce. In the event that either spouse shall hereafter obtain a decree of divorce, all of the covenants, terms and provisions of this Agreement shall

survive the same and continue in full force and effect and without limiting the generality of the foregoing, neither party shall have or assert any cause of action in tort against the other.

15. EXECUTION OF OTHER DOCUMENTS: The husband and wife shall at any time and from time to time execute and deliver to the other any document or documents that the other reasonably requires to give effect to the terms of this Agreement.

16. SEVERABILITY: The invalidity of any section of this Agreement does not affect the validity of the other sections, and the husband and the wife specifically agree that each and every paragraph of this Agreement shall be severable from the other.

17. DISCLOSURE: The parties acknowledge that they have been fully advised and informed of the income, estate and prospects of the other party and have been fully advised and informed by their solicitors of their respective rights and liabilities against and to each other to and with reference to the income, property and estate of the other.

18. INDEPENDENT LEGAL ADVICE: The husband and wife each acknowledge that each,

(a) has had independent legal advice;

(b) understands their respective rights and obligations under this Agreement; and

(c) is signing this Separation Agreement voluntarily.

19. WIFE'S LEGAL FEES AND DISBURSEMENTS: The husband shall reimburse the wife for all legal fees and disbursements incurred by her in engaging the services of N. E. One, Barrister and Solicitor, for the negotiation and preparation of this Agreement.

IN WITNESS WHEREOF the husband and the wife hereunto set their hands and seals.

SIGNED, SEALED AND DELIVERED in the presence of:		
______________________ (witness)	)	______________________ JANE DOE
______________________ (witness)	)	______________________ JOHN DOE

GLOSSARY

Co-respondent: a person with whom a respondent is alleged to have committed adultery.
Decree nisi: a judge's order granting a divorce.
"Deserted wives" legislation: laws in Alberta, Saskatchewan, New Brunswick, Nova Scotia, Newfoundland and the Yukon and Northwest Territories that provide support for a wife who has been "deserted" according to a specific definition. Also called "fault" or matrimonial misconduct legislation.
Dependant: a person to whom another has an obligation to provide support.
Family assets: In Ontario, Prince Edward Island and British Columbia and Manitoba, certain items are defined, largely by their use, as family assets when a couple separates, and are subject to a specific method of division.
Marriage breakdown: a group of grounds for divorce that includes three- or five-year separation, gross addiction to alcohol or narcotics and non-consummation.
Matrimonial offences: a group of grounds for divorce that includes adultery, cruelty and homosexuality.
"No-fault" legislation: laws in Ontario, Prince Edward Island, British Columbia and Manitoba that provide support after separation on the basis of largely economic criteria.
Petitioner: the spouse who applies for a divorce.
Respondent: the spouse being sued for divorce.
Separate property system: system of property under which each spouse has the right to use and dispose of property to which he or she has title or other interest.
Service: delivery of a divorce petition or other legal papers.

Born and raised in Sudbury, Lynn King now practises law in Toronto where she concentrates on family law and women's rights. She has been active in women's organizations pressing for reforms in the laws relating to marriage and divorce.